STIMULATING SEX—
IT'S AS MUCH A HEAD GAME
AS IT IS A BODY SPORT

The couples in this book frankly reveal how the sexual fantasies they create together—and act out—give them the kind of sexual fulfillment many couples only dream of. In mastering these sensual techniques, you and your partner will learn how the mind games you play add a delicious dimension to sex that stirs and satisfies your erotic appetites. As this book vividly shows, there is nothing forbidden in what couples do, say, and think in the privacy of their passion—and no limits to the pleasures they can explore and enjoy when they give free rein to their deepest desires and wildest imaginations. Let this exciting introduction to gloriously inventive lovemaking prove to you that the most thrilling erogenous zone of all is your mind!

IRIS and STEVEN FINZ are the authors of over 100 adult novels. Steven Finz is, in addition, a law professor teaching in Southern California. They currently make their home in Dulzura, California.

Whispered Secrets

The Couple's Guide to Erotic Fantasy

Iris and Steven Finz

A SIGNET BOOK

NEW AMERICAN LIBRARY

A DIVISION OF PENGUIN BOOKS USA INC.

NAL BOOKS ARE AVAILABLE AT QUANTITY DISCOUNTS WHEN USED
TO PROMOTE PRODUCTS OR SERVICES. FOR INFORMATION PLEASE
WRITE TO PREMIUM MARKETING DIVISION, NEW AMERICAN LIBRARY,
1633 BROADWAY, NEW YORK, NEW YORK 10019.

SIGNET, SIGNET CLASSIC, MENTOR, ONYX, PLUME, MERIDIAN and
NAL BOOKS are published by New American Library, a division of Penguin
Books USA Inc., 1633 Broadway, New York, New York 10019

First Printing, February, 1990

1 2 3 4 5 6 7 8 9

PRINTED IN THE UNITED STATES OF AMERICA

To love and sex . . .
They belong together.

Contents

Introduction

Iris and I began sharing our fantasies when we were too young to be embarrassed about them. We met when we were twelve and began playing adolescent sex games by the time we were fourteen. Fantasy became part of those games right from the start.

One day, while kissing and necking in the park, Iris whispered, "We're being held prisoner, and the people who captured us are watching."

I added, "They'll let us go, but only if they like what they see us doing."

For the rest of the afternoon, we weren't just petting; we were performing for an imaginary audience.

That was in 1957. Four years later, we ran off to get married. We've been together for more than twenty-seven years since then and are still enriching our relationship with shared fantasies. These whispered daydreams of ours have made it possible for us to experience every possible erotic delight without risking our health, our safety, or the emotional stability of our marriage.

Although we have an extensive repertoire of erotic fantasies, we still replay that first one from time to time while making love. It's more complex now, of course. We've embellished and elaborated on it over the years. Like us, it has become more sophisticated. We know who our imaginary captors are, and we know what they look like. We know what sexual acts they want to watch, and we know how to please them so that they'll set us free. Sometimes our fantasy-jailers even get into bed with us.

In the beginning, we thought our whispered exchange of secrets was unique. But now we know better. We have met many couples who bring variety to their sex lives by pretending or imagining, making fantasy a regular part of their erotic play. Most keep their games a secret, unaware that others like them are playing similar games. We, too, might have remained unaware, if not for the eroticism in our professional activities.

To help finance my studies in law school, Iris and I began writing adult novels in 1968. Over the years, we published more than a hundred of them. Frequently, these were based on the fantasies we had developed together.

After completing school, I practiced law for a while. At the same time, both of us continued writing, making sexuality our literary specialty. While Iris wrote romance fiction, I wrote magazine columns on sex and the law.

A few years later, I quit practicing law and began teaching it. Today I am a professor of law at a university in San Diego, California, and a free-lance lecturer. I also teach on a nationwide basis for a company that offers courses to law graduates. Although we stopped writing adult fiction when I started teaching law, we never lost our professional interest in human sexuality. I have often lectured to psychologists and other mental-health professionals on the legal aspects of sexuality, and to law students on the legal regulation of pornography.

Somehow this led the people around us to think of us as experts on the erotic—professionals to whom they could confess their deepest sex secrets. Frequently, they approached us to talk about sexual subjects. As conversations became more intimate, we were surprised to learn that other husbands and wives also pretend and fantasize together while making love. At first we listened, incredulous, to these unexpected revelations, simply absorbing the fact that the game we thought we invented wasn't ours alone.

After a while we conceived the idea of this book— an anthology of sexual fantasies shared by loving couples. We started collecting these fantasies as friends and acquaintances described them to us. With their permission, we took notes and even tape-recorded some of these descriptions for inclusion in our book.

Sometimes we met with resistance from people who feared that admitting to a fantasy life would expose them to ridicule or embarrassment. When we told them about the book's point of view, however, the resistance usually melted. This is a book about the fantasies of sexually successful couples. The people who reported them to us have no reason to be ashamed or embarrassed, because they have succeeded where others have failed. They are all people who have found ways to make their relationships work.

For obvious reasons, we have changed the names of the people involved. We have also done a little editing to assure continuity. Otherwise, these really are the whispered secrets of happy couples.

1 Whispered Secrets

This is a book about fantasy. In its broadest sense, "fantasy" is simply another name for "imagination"—the mind's ability to visualize. Since humans are the only creatures on earth to have imagination, fantasy is a uniquely human experience.

The commercial importance of this phenomenon is obvious. All works of fiction—whether printed in books and magazines, recorded on film and videotape, or acted out on stages—start out as someone's fantasies. So, whenever we entertain ourselves by reading a novel or seeing a play, we are making another person's fantasy part of our own lives.

Fantasies serve purposes other than entertainment, however. Psychiatrist Theodore Reik equated fantasy with curiosity, suggesting that we fantasize about the things we would like to know. When a man wonders how it would be to make love to two women at the same time, he will probably imagine it. A woman who is curious about whether her tennis instructor is a good lover may daydream about lying in his arms.

Modern psychologists say that people also use their fantasies to resolve emotional problems. A woman who hates her job may escape from the frustrating reality it represents by retreating into a dream world filled with romance and freedom. A man who fears his boss may reduce his anxieties by imagining life aboard a sailboat headed for the Polynesian islands. A person who lacks a loving partner may satisfy real needs by thinking of a favorite movie star while masturbating.

Since our curiosity, our frustrations, our anxieties, and our needs are frequently sexual, many of our fantasies are about sex. Freud said that our sexual fantasies begin in the cradle, but that shame causes us to repress the memory of them when we reach adulthood. This is not usually true of the fantasies we have in adolescence. Most men can remember gazing at a teacher's breasts while in high school and thinking of how they would look without a bra and blouse to cover them. Most women can recall erotic schoolgirl daydreams about older boys they knew in their early teens.

As a result, many of us think of fantasy as an aspect of adolescence. We expect teenagers to have daydreams. We believe that healthy imaginations help prepare kids for the future. On the other hand, we tend to think that it's not quite right for an adult to fantasize, describing those who do in terms of mild disapproval. We don't usually think as much of an adult who is a "dreamer" with "head in the clouds" as of a "doer" with "feet on the ground." We characterize adult fantasies as pipe dreams, as if to suggest that they are drug-induced. In these ways we express the belief that right-thinking adults do not fantasize.

This, of course, is far from the truth. All adults fantasize, particularly about sex. Some psychiatrists say that erotic fantasy is the most common of all sexual phenomena. This difference between our true sexuality and our belief about how our sexuality should be causes most of us to hide our sexual fantasies from those around us. Often, we hide them even from ourselves.

Although a showing of X-rated fantasy is playing continuously to some level of our subconscious minds, we are usually unaware of the performance. On occasion, it may intrude, without permission, into our consciousness. A man riding on a bus may experience an unsolicited flight of fancy that requires him to hide a sudden and unbidden erection by crossing his legs. While sitting in a dentist's waiting room, a woman may raise a magazine to cover the stiffening of taut nipples induced by an unwilling journey into erotic imagination.

Much of the time, adult sex fantasies are kept secret. The results of a recently published survey indicated that 87 percent of the people who admitted having sex fantasies believed that their partners would respond unfavorably if they found out about them. Nancy Friday, who has done extensive research on the subject of adult sex fantasies, published three books filled with statements by informants of both genders who were certain that if their lovers or mates knew about their fantasies they would be hurt or angry or worse.

Ms. Friday began one of those books by describing her own experience along these lines. While she and a partner were making love, she was fantasizing about having sex with a stranger at a football game. Suddenly, her partner asked what she was thinking. She says that when she told him, her lover "got out of bed, put on his pants, and went home."

For many people, fantasy serves to fill the gaps in a disappointing sex life. In hopes of procuring an otherwise unavailable orgasm, some women secretly enjoy fantasy lovers while their husbands thrust at them ineptly. To spice uninspired marital couplings, some men clandestinely imagine that they are being fondled by nude strangers on a public beach while their wives lie motionless beneath them. They wouldn't think of telling their mates about their fantasies. To do so would be to express dissatisfaction.

But there is another side to adult sexual fantasy. Many happy couples make shared fantasy a legitimate part of their life together. While making love, they become partners in imagination, using fantasy scenarios to heighten their excitement. Instead of hiding bitter daydreams in the solitude of introspection, they whisper delightful secrets into each other's ears. Sometimes, they develop favorites, polishing and refining these standby fantasies over the years as they grow together sexually. A husband learns what special imaginary events please his wife and finds that talking about them pleases him as well. A wife discovers that certain thoughts excite her husband and that sharing those thoughts excites her too. Thus they use their imaginations in concert to enhance reality rather than to escape from it.

If one of them has a secret yearning to have sex with a stranger at a football game, they indulge that yearning together. They create the stranger and the stadium in mutual fantasy and bring it all into the marital bed so that both can enjoy the imaginary infidelity. A woman who dreams of having another woman or of having ten men at a time can share that dream with her mate, delighting in it without shame or risk. A man who longs for the pleasures of a harem can ask his wife to help him build one. She can even assist him in filling it with the exotic women of his dreams, so long as he shares those dreams with her. For a variety of reasons, their garden of dreams may be a secret from the rest of the world. But in the privacy of their relationship, they whisper these secrets to each other, sharing the uniquely human pleasures of their joint imagination.

Some believe that the joys they experience in fantasy have made their relationships stronger. Some say that if not for the imaginary affairs that they have enjoyed with their spouses, they would have destroyed their marriages long ago with real affairs. Some even feel that the closeness that has resulted from their games of sexual make-believe makes it easier for them to solve the nonsexual problems that arise in every relationship.

There are probably some people who will find deep meanings hidden in the fantasies our couples described: latencies, repressions, and Lord knows what else. Others may find it significant that more of the fantasies contained in this book were described by women than by men. We are content to leave the psychological and sociological analysis to those who are expert in those fields and who think that such analysis serves some purpose. What we offer here is a collection of the erotic fantasies that some sexually successful couples share to enrich and invigorate their intimate moments. It works for them. It can work for you.

If you and your mate are willing to try something new and would like to experience passions that have yet to be discovered, sexual fantasy can be the vehicle that takes you to uncharted levels of fulfillment. You already know some of the things that excite your partner, and your partner knows some of the things that get you aroused. Use this knowledge to start creating your mutual fantasy. Then relax your inhibitions enough to let the fantasy evolve by itself. In doing so, you'll learn more about each other and you'll achieve heights of sexual satisfaction that you've never known before.

2

Ah, Yes,
I Remember It Well

Memories can be our most precious treasures. Once formed, they are with us forever. Although we don't remember everything, most psychologists agree that we don't really forget anything. Our memory, they say, is a warehouse that contains everything we ever saw, heard, or experienced. Sometimes we cause ourselves to block those memories that are unpleasant or threatening, but those that give us pleasure can usually be recalled whenever we want or need them.

There is great comfort in knowing that no matter what happens to our material possessions, we will always have our memories. When things don't go the way we hoped they would, recollections of better times are there to soften the blows. There is room for the remembrance of things past, even in the happiest of lives.

Every time we retreat into the world of memory, we are fantasizing. In recalling the high-school prom or the night of our first date, we are visualizing things that are not happening now. We are experiencing or reexperiencing them in our imagination. This is the most basic form of fantasy.

A survey recently published in the *The Journal of Sex Research* found that for two out of every three people studied, the most common sex fantasy was based on the memory of an actual sexual encounter. Our own research indicates that the percentage may be even higher, because many people who enjoy reliving pleasant sexual memories don't realize that they are fantasizing. Whenever one of the couples we interviewed denied sharing fantasies, we would ask if they ever talk to each other about past sex experiences. Almost always, the answer was ''Yes.''

Some said that their favorite memories concerned significant events in the development of their relationships. Others said that they enjoy sharing recollections of occasions when their lovemaking was especially erotic or when they had the most fun. All have learned to sharpen the memories—to dwell on the most arousing parts, to embellish the remembered details, to freely add new ones. For them, the process of sharing erotic thoughts has become a sexual activity in itself, providing a spice that enlivens their other sex acts.

We chose to open this book with fantasies based on memories because everybody has them. If you and your mate ever talked to each other about a sexual experience that you had together, you were sharing an erotic fantasy, perhaps without even knowing it. If so, welcome to the world of whispered secrets.

KAREN AND GILES

Iris:

When Steve and I were in our early teens, we belonged to a circle of friends that met a few afternoons a week to watch *American Bandstand* on TV and to dance. It was fashionable to go steady, so most of the kids in the group had formed into couples. At our afternoon get-togethers, we would usually end up "making out." At the time, this meant anything from hugs and kisses to heavy petting, depending how long a particular couple had been going steady. Because there would be six or eight couples making out in the same room at the same time, a certain intimacy developed among members of the group.

Some of the friendships formed during that period have never ended. Recently, while Steve was lecturing to a class of law graduates in New York City, I looked up Karen, one of our old friends from those adolescent days. Although Karen and I hadn't seen each other in more than fifteen years, we occasionally corresponded and spoke on the telephone.

We met outside the lecture hall and took a cab to a posh Manhattan restaurant. We ordered an elegant dinner, and the wine flowed freely. After Karen brought me up to date on her life and her work, I told her that Steve and I were writing a book about couples' sexual fantasies.

"Wow," she exploded with the unabashed enthusiasm for which she had been known as a teenager. "You absolutely must include mine and Giles'. You absolutely must. It's all about the first time we ever really did it. That was years ago, but we still talk about it whenever we want to get really turned on . . ."

* * *

Do you remember our last year of high school when Gloria threw that big New Year's Eve party. Giles and I showed up, but we left almost immediately. We had decided to rent a hotel room, and the party gave us a perfect alibi. Our parents were always giving us a hard time about staying out late, but this was New Year's Eve and they knew about Gloria's party, so it was all right. We told them that the kids were all planning to ride the Staten Island ferry in the morning to watch the sun come up, and then we were all going to have breakfast together somewhere. So they didn't expect us home until the middle of the next day.

You remember all the making out we used to do in those days. God, we used to kiss and neck for hours. Giles and I had done almost everything already, but we hadn't gone all the way. And we really didn't have any intention of doing it that night. But we were really excited because this was going to be the first time that we were actually going to sleep together in the same bed and wake up with one another.

We planned for it a week in advance. Giles even bought a cheap wedding band for me to wear so that the hotel clerk wouldn't suspect anything. Giles had gotten two bottles of champagne, and I took some food from Gloria's party, knowing that she'd never miss it. We were ready for our own party.

The hotel room was quite nice, but that wasn't

really what we were interested in. As soon as we got into the room, Giles opened one of the bottles and poured champagne. We were already a little high from the vodka punch we drank at Gloria's party, and excited to be in our very own hotel room. As we sipped the champagne from the plastic hotel glasses, I sat on Giles' lap and we started to kiss.

Well, you remember how that was. Before long, he had his hand inside my blouse and was feeling me up through my bra. We were so used to making out with a crowd around us that it took a while for us to realize that we were free to do whatever we wanted. I said, "Why don't you take it off me?" And he did, unbuttoning the blouse with one hand while he was still feeling my breasts with the other. My nipples were so hard I thought they would burn holes in my bra.

I wanted to take everything off, so I stood up and removed my skirt. I started to pull down my half-slip, but Giles stopped me. He said that he wanted to look at me like that for a while. He sat back in the hotel chair and just stared while I turned around in a circle.

It wasn't the first time he had seen me in my slip and bra. Sometimes, when my parents were out, we'd fool around at my house. But we were always worried about getting caught, and this night we didn't have anything to worry about at all. We were really enjoying the feeling of freedom.

After a while I took off the slip and stood there in my bra and panties while he looked. I was wearing really brief bikinis, flesh-colored. Even though my pubic hair is blond, I knew that he could see it through the material because I had put them on and looked at myself in the mirror lots of times.

It made me excited to see how hard he was staring at me. But then I wanted to see him too. So I told him to stand up and take off everything but his underwear. Oooh, it was something. His penis was so hard that it stood straight out in front of him, stretching the fabric of his white shorts. And his pouch made a sexy bulge.

We put our arms around each other and pressed our bodies together while his tongue went deep into my mouth. He's taller than me, so I could feel his penis pressing against my belly. I wiggled a little to rub my breasts against his chest.

His fingers were trembling as they worked to unhook my bra. To this day I get a wild sensation just thinking about how it felt when he finally got it open and my breasts tumbled out. He tossed the bra to the floor and moved himself back and forth, stroking my nipples with the hair on his chest. Then he stepped back and looked me up and down like he had never seen me before. Bending forward, he flicked the tip of his tongue over my nipples.

When I put my hand inside his underpants, I was amazed at how warm and smooth the skin of his penis was. I had felt it before, of course, but this was different. It felt like a living creature, throbbing and pulsing with a life of its own. I wanted to feel it against my skin, so I pulled his shorts down and told him to take off my panties. For a while we continued to stand there, rubbing our bodies together. The moisture oozing from the tip of his penis was leaving hot wet trails on my belly. I could feel my vagina puckering open, and suddenly I wanted to feel him inside of me. So I said, "Let's lie down and get comfortable."

The rules were different in those days. Boys were supposed to respect girls, and that meant that no matter how much petting and fooling around went on there wasn't supposed to be any penetration. We had been naked together before and we had lain together with his penis up against me, but we had never had real intercourse. Once in a while he rubbed the tip of his penis against my pubic hair. And on a few occasions, he even placed it right up against the lips of my opening. But it had never been inside.

When I lay back on the bed, I spread my legs wide apart so that he would have a good clear view of my open vagina. "Why don't you put it in me just a little bit," I said. "Just the head."

At this point, Giles got nervous. After all, we weren't supposed to actually do it until we were married or at least engaged. He said that it was his job to make sure that we didn't do something we'd both regret in the morning, and he started licking my nipples, hoping I wouldn't mention it again.

But I reached down and grabbed his penis in my hand, pulling on it until it was positioned right against the lips of my vagina. By now I was so wet that the contact caused a kissing sound that excited me even more. "Come on," I whispered. "Just put the head of it into my opening. I won't let you go in too deep. We'll both know when you reach my cherry. And we won't go any further."

Giles didn't feel completely right about it, but I could tell by his heavy breathing that he was too excited to think rationally. So, without actually agreeing to anything, he let me guide the tip of his erection into my open slit. I'll never forget the way that first entry felt. I don't think I've been that wet before or since. But I was. so tight that I felt like I was being forced open. I thought his organ must be the biggest in the world.

In my excitement, I started to lift my hips up off the bed to drive him deeper inside. But this made him worried, and he pulled back and out as if he had been burned with an iron. I felt so empty now that I started to beg him to put it back inside. He still said no, but all his resistance was gone.

This time, it slipped a little easier. I was very conscious that the membranes of my vagina were wrapped completely around his swollen penis. I wanted a little more. And then a little more. He was filling me with that thick wonderful pole, and I wanted it all.

All the muscles of Giles' arms and back were tense as he held his weight up off me. I ground my hips around in little circles, trying to ease the tightness. I was starting to feel a pain in the hidden recesses of my vagina, and it seemed like the only thing that would make it go away was to have him deeper inside me. I pushed up against him and felt him draw back slightly, trying to avoid shattering my hymen.

In spite of the pain, nothing had ever felt so good before. I was afraid that he would slip out of me. So I suddenly threw my pelvis up at him, driving his penis in to the hilt. We were rocking together in the rhythm of intercourse before either of us realized that my virginity was a thing of the past. Once we did realize it, there was nothing we could do but just keep on humping.

Giles came, of course, but I didn't. When it was over, there were tears in his eyes and he started to apologize. "I didn't mean for it to happen this way," he said. "I always wanted to wait until we were married."

I was on the verge of crying too, partially at the idea of losing my virginity and partially at the pain I was feeling in my womb. But then I reached for his penis and found that it was hard again. And without realizing what I was doing, I pulled him back onto me and guided it to my vagina once more.

This time Giles didn't hesitate. He shoved it in all the way on the very first thrust, then lay still to give my tight vagina a chance to adjust. Instinctively, we started to move apart and together, pulling his penis almost out of me and then driving it in to the hilt again. I could feel the tension in my vaginal muscles relaxing, and the fit wasn't quite so tight. We kept moving that way until I felt an orgasm coming.

Before that, Giles sometimes made me come with his finger, but no climax ever felt like this one. It seemed like there were circular ripples starting at my groin and spreading throughout my entire body. I started to sob even before I came, and for a moment I thought that I would not be able to catch my breath. Then it began. Wave after wave of ecstasy crashed over me, and I cried out in rhythm to the contractions of my body. Giles came again, filling me with his semen until it overflowed and made a puddle on the bedsheet.

We got married a year later, and we've always had

good sex. But I don't think it has ever been as good as it was that night. Sometimes, when we want to relive it, we start talking about it while undressing for bed. Then, without any foreplay, Giles climbs on top of me and puts his penis against my vaginal lips. If I'm dry, it feels tight, almost like it did that first time.

We pretend we're back in that hotel room. I say, "Just put the tip of it in my opening. I won't let you go in too deep. Just let me feel the head inside me."

Giles says, "I don't think we should. I don't want to break your cherry." Then he rams it in while I'm still dry so that my vagina pulls tight around him. We hump slowly, talking like we did that first time. Then, when we feel my juices flowing, we screw like mad until we come together.

NATALIE AND HERB

Steve:

Natalie and Herb think of themselves as Yuppies. She is a dental hygienist in her early thirties. He is an oral surgeon about the same age. We've never met Herb, but we see Natalie twice a year or so. One day after she finished working on my teeth, she said that Iris had mentioned that we were working on a book about the fantasies of happy couples and that the idea intrigued her.

"I told Herb about it," she added. "And he thought you might like to hear about our favorite fantasy. Actually, it's based on something that really happened to us. Does that count? It was about six years ago, before we got married . . ."

* * *

Herb was in dental school at the time and I was still in college. Neither of us had much money, but Herb had a beat-up old car. And, boy, did that car see a lot of action! I shared an apartment with three other girls, and Herb had five roommates, making it impossible for us to go to his place or mine. We were too poor to rent a hotel room, so it was the car or nothing. We used to park in all sorts of places and climb into the backseat to neck. But when we could scrape up five dollars, we would go to the drive-in movies.

This particular drive-in used to run a special during the week. Five bucks a carload—the cheapest date in town. Usually, they would show two grade-B movies and a bunch of cartoons. But that wasn't really what we went for. We might watch a little of the movie, but mostly we went there to make out in the backseat of the car.

We'd try to get there early so that we could pick the most secluded corner of the drive-in and be sure of having some privacy. We always parked far away from the food concession and rest rooms so that nobody would be walking past our car and looking in.

This particular night we had a little extra money, so we brought a bottle of wine with us and two paper cups. Ever drink wine out of a paper cup? Awful. Just awful.

Anyway, we drank the wine and watched the cartoons. Then, when the first feature began, we got into the backseat for a spot of heavy breathing. Truth is, we were both feeling the wine and acting kind of giddy. I think we actually forgot where we were.

We started to kiss, and pretty soon Herb had his hands inside my blouse and I was all twisted up in my bra. I was getting real excited, but the straps were cutting into my shoulders, so I just slid out of them. This turned Herb into a hungry beast. He was kissing me all over and biting me and nibbling me. I still get little chills just thinking about it.

Anyway, after a while I wanted to fondle him, too. So I opened his belt and unzipped his pants and started feeling around trying to get my hand on it. But he was wearing boxer shorts, and they were all tangled up. So he shoved his pants and underpants down and pushed them off with his feet.

By now, of course, the movie was forgotten and we were having a grand old time. It was a real cloudy night, and the drive-in was half-empty. We felt like we were the only people in the whole world. After a while, I had my head in Herb's lap and I could feel him getting hotter and hotter. It seemed like the hotter he got, the hotter I got.

We weren't exactly virgins, but we hadn't done it too many times, mainly because it was so hard to find any privacy. All I knew was that this night, I really wanted it. I guess the wine was working on me, filling me with that warm and tingly feeling that's so hard to resist.

Without taking my mouth away from Herb, I managed to slip out of my pants and panties. I don't even think Herb knew I was doing it. By now, of course,

I'm completely naked, and he's not wearing anything but a shirt.

I sat up straight and turned to straddle his lap, facing him. He caressed me while we kissed. I reached down and put him in me. He was so hard that I couldn't think of anything else. My eyes were closed tight, but I could imagine the sight of him sliding in.

He was playing with my breasts and rubbing the sensitive spots. And we were rocking back and forth to drive him in and out of me. The whole car must have been shaking, but we were oblivious.

I was sobbing and moaning, and so was Herb. It must have been plenty loud, but of course, we were the only people in the world, so it never occurred to us that anyone else could hear it. When I felt a climax hitting me, I positively shouted, "Oh, Herb, I'm going to come."

He said, "Me too."

Just as he said it, my orgasm began. I opened my eyes to see him. He opened his eyes at the same time. And then I saw an expression of horror come over his face. I turned to see what he was looking at, and, boy, was I shocked.

It seems we had collected an audience. All the people in the cars around us were looking at us. Some had even gotten out of their cars and were standing outside staring right into our windows for a better look. Nobody was bothering with the picture on the big screen. Why should they? They had a better show, live and in person.

We were out of control now. How do you stop an

orgasm? There was nothing we could do but come. And come. And come. It seemed to go on forever.

I wanted to close my eyes again and retreat back into the illusion of privacy. But it was impossible. As my climax overpowered me, I just looked around at the fascinated faces of our uninvited audience. Herb had the same problem. I could feel him throbbing and swelling inside of me as he ejaculated, but his eyes were wide open and staring back at all the lookers.

I'll tell you, the feeling was intense. But it's the only time in my life that I can remember wishing for an orgasm to end. When it was over, I said, ''Herb, get me out of here.''

I never knew Herb could move so quickly. Grabbing his pants, he climbed over into the front seat, opened the window just far enough to unhook the drive-in speaker, and tossed it onto the ground. He covered himself as best he could by throwing his crumpled-up pants over his lap, started the engine, and shifted into gear all in one swift motion.

I didn't even try to get dressed, but just rolled myself into a ball on the backseat, trying to shield my nakedness from all those eyes. I remember hearing cheers and applause as we drove out.

Our getaway annoyed the few people who didn't catch our show and were actually watching the screen. Our tires were squealing. We kept going until we reached a dark dead-end street and stopped to put our clothes back on. By now we were laughing so hard that we couldn't control ourselves. And we kept laughing until the evening ended.

To this day, whenever either of us is feeling a little

playful, we talk about that evening. You might say that Herb and I use our memory of it to get ourselves turned on. Instead of remembering the embarrassment we felt, we just remember the fun and the excitement of having that colossal orgasm while an audience of strangers looked on. Discussing it like that never fails to get to us.

Sometimes I talk about it while we make love, describing it to Herb from my point of view—how it felt to be completely naked with him inside of me while a group of strangers watched appreciatively. I elaborate, of course. I can describe in detail the faces of the men who saw me naked and watched me climax, even though, at the time, I know I couldn't have paid any attention to those details.

Sometimes Herb does the talking, telling me what he saw them doing—the men and the women—while they watched us. He tells me what they were saying, even what they were thinking as they saw us screwing there in the backseat of his car. That's the nice thing about fantasy. You can make it do anything you want.

HAL AND SHARON

Iris:

Hal and Sharon are registered nurses specializing in mental health. They are in their mid-twenties and have been seeing each other for two years. Although they maintain separate apartments, they sleep together almost every night, sometimes at her place, sometimes at his.

The laws of their state require health-care professionals to continue their education by regularly taking courses on subjects related to their work. For this reason, they attended one of Steve's lectures on sex and the law. I happened to be seated in the audience near Sharon and Hal, and during one of the breaks we struck up a conversation. Steve had been speaking on the legal penalties for exhibitionism.

Hal caught my interest when he said that he and Sharon owed a lot to a pair of exhibitionists they once saw in New York. I was dying to hear the details, so after Steve's lecture, I insisted they join us for a cup of coffee. As soon as I could do so gracefully, I asked Hal to explain his remark. He and Sharon seemed as eager to tell it as we were to hear it. They both spoke, sometimes simultaneously, sometimes interrupting each other. To avoid confusion, I'm setting their words down as if Hal did all the talking.

"We've always loved talking about sex while we make love," he began. "But in the beginning we both felt a little awkward about it. Then we saw something through a window in New York that really gave us something to talk about. Since then, it's been easy . . ."

* * *

About a year and a half ago, I decided to show Sharon New York. I grew up there, you know, but it was Sharon's first time in the Big Apple. I reserved us a room on the sixth floor of a hotel right in the heart of midtown Manhattan so she could really get the feel of the place. It wasn't the classiest hotel in town, but it was in the center of all that big-city bustle. I thought Sharon would get a kick out of watching the action in the street below our window. What happened, though, was that we spent most of our time watching the action in a window across the street.

New York is a crazy place. The building across from our hotel was several stories high. The ground level and a floor or two above it contained a factory of some kind—garments, I think. During the day we could look through the windows to see machines operating and workers running back and forth with bundles of fabric in their arms. At five o'clock the lights went out and the place emptied out.

But one evening, noticing lights on in a fourth-floor window, we realized that there was an apartment up there. The idea puzzled us, and we stood at the window of our hotel room for a while just looking in. The apartment seemed to be furnished with some affluence, even though it was located over a factory. Then I saw a movement through the window. I said something to Sharon about it, something like, ''Hey, there's somebody walking around in there.''

Sharon had already seen. ''I know,'' she said. ''I've been watching her. She doesn't have any clothes on.''

The minute she said it, I realized that she was right. The woman in the window was tall, with pale white skin and long dark hair. And she wasn't wearing a stitch. I couldn't see her face very well, but I could see her body. She had big round tits and a dark bush of pubic hair. I could feel myself getting hard and was a little ashamed, thinking that Sharon would take me for a pervert if she knew. But I just couldn't tear my eyes away from the window.

A moment later I realized that there was a man there also. He was almost naked too, wearing nothing but a pair of white brief shorts. Then he pulled them down and kicked them off. His cock was long and hard, and when it sprang into view, I heard Sharon draw her breath in sharply.

By now I had a full erection, but I wasn't the least bit ashamed anymore. In fact, I took Sharon's hand and put it right on the front of my pants. She played with me for a moment and then unzipped my fly, her eyes still glued to the erotic scene across the street.

The sill of the window at which we were standing was about waist-high. So I knew that if I took off my pants, nobody outside would be able to see anything. Quickly, I unbuckled my belt and dropped my pants and shorts. Then, stepping out of them, I moved behind Sharon. I pulled up her skirt until it was around her waist and began rubbing my erection against her panties. When she started grinding her ass back against me, I drew the panties down to her ankles and slipped them off her feet.

By now the couple across the street were embracing. I could see his hands moving over her ass and her breasts, and I could see him humping forward to press the tip of his penis against her crotch. Sharon started moving rhythmically backwards and forwards. It felt like she was trying to match her movements to those of the other two people. "Do you think they know we're watching?" she asked. "Do you think they can see us?'' The idea seemed to turn her on even more than what they were doing.

Reaching inside her blouse to fondle her breasts, I said, ''Sure they do. In fact, they're putting on a show just for us.''

At this point, I could feel Sharon start to tremble all over. She gripped my penis between her bare thighs as she swayed without once taking her eyes off the couple in the window. The woman had sunk to her knees in front of the man and had taken his penis in her mouth. Sharon was fascinated. I reached around and cupped both her breasts, feeling Sharon's hand moving between her legs from in front to take hold of me and guide me into her. She bent her knees slightly and sighed as I penetrated her from behind.

We stood in the window that way for a long time, screwing slowly while we watched the woman in the apartment giving her man a blowjob. From their movements, it looked like he was going to climax any second. His hips were moving powerfully back and forth, driving his erection into her bobbing face. Finally, he stopped moving and she let his penis slip out of her mouth. He said something to her, and then they both looked at us and seemed to smile. I'm almost certain that the naked woman's eyes met mine. When they moved off to the back of their apartment, we lost sight of them.

But Sharon and I didn't stop. We stood that way for another hour, grinding our bodies together and pretending that we could still see them. Every once in a while, one of us would describe them as if they were still making love in front of the window. Neither of us wanted it to end, so whenever one of us was close to coming, we slowed down or stopped moving completely. When we couldn't hold back any longer, we came—both at the same time. Neither of us ever had such a strong orgasm before.

Since then, whenever we're staying at a hotel out of town we make love in front of the window. Usually, we do it the same way we did it in New York, with both of us covered from the waist up but naked below the level of the windowsill. Each time we do it, we talk about the couple in the window. We like to imagine that they knew we were watching. We've spent many hours fantasizing about what it must have felt like for them to put on a show for us that way. But mostly, we like to remember how aroused we both got that night in New York.

3   Lie with Me in the Grass

Western civilization has always regarded sex as something nice people don't do out of doors. The ancient Greeks extolled the beauty of nature, but were careful not to encourage sex under the sun and sky. Although their athletes competed nude in huge open-air arenas, propriety required that the men be uncircumcised so that the heads of their penises would always be hidden from sight.

When the ancient Romans adopted the Greeks' admiration for the glories of nature, they ignored most Greek inhibitions except those relating to outdoor sex. In A.D. 40, the Roman philosopher Seneca referred to a certain summer resort as "the haven of the vices," because lovers were known to have intercourse on the beaches there. The Roman government considered al fresco orgies—known as Bacchanalia—a threat to the republic, and sometimes put participants to death.

During Western civilization's Dark Ages, when Roman philosophy gave way to Christianity, all sex was banished to a place behind closed doors, where it has remained ever since. Eastern poetry treats "a book of verse beneath the bough, a loaf of bread, a jug of wine, and thou beside me in the wilderness'' as perfect ingredients for a love tryst. To the Western mind, however, these are the makings of a picnic and nothing more.

On a summer day, the sensuous prospect of feeling warm breeze against bare skin may draw us to the seashore even when we don't feel like swimming. But though our bathing suits are brief, we keep them on. That's as close as most Americans ever come to outdoor nudity.

On the beaches of Europe, the rules are slightly more permissive. Although complete nudity is verboten in many places, women are almost always permitted to sunbathe without tops on so that they can tan evenly. There are always some who continue to lie topless on their blankets long after the air cools and the sun goes down. It must give them a deliciously naughty feeling.

Since forbidden fruit is usually the sweetest, many people dream about outdoor sex. The 1953 movie *From Here to Eternity* received several Academy Award nominations including Best Director, Best Film, Best Actor, Best Actress, Best Supporting Actor, and Best Supporting Actress. But the scene everybody remembers best is the one in which Burt Lancaster and Deborah Kerr made love on a moonlit beach amid the crashing of ocean waves. In spite of the movie industry's code, which required actors to wear bathing suits, the suggestion of outdoor sex made the shot intensely erotic.

For most couples, out-of-doors sex will never be a reality. They'll think about it; they'll talk about it; they'll imagine it. But they won't ever do it, because their inhibitions, their society, and their belief systems all tell them they shouldn't. That's probably why outdoor sex is a favorite fantasy among many of the couples we interviewed. Their imaginations let them experience what they otherwise could not. After all, that's what fantasies are for.

LIZ AND BEN

Iris:

Liz and I worked as junior counselors together at a summer camp when we were both in our teens. In fact, Liz met her husband, Ben, there. While at camp, Liz and I shared a cabin. As a result, we developed the kind of friendship that adolescent girls form so easily. We talked frequently to each other about the intimate details of our budding love lives.

Our friendship has continued to this day. Now, whenever we see each other, we can't help but talk of old times and the camp experiences we shared. Recently, after we had dinner together, I mentioned the fun we used to have swimming in the lake at camp every afternoon. I was puzzled when Liz smiled and said that she and Ben returned to the lake frequently.

"Really?" I asked.

"Well, in a manner of speaking," Liz answered. "You might say we were there just a few days ago . . ."

* * *

Ben and I spent a lot of time down by the lake that summer. Especially at night. Most evenings there were campfires or planned activities in the recreation hall, and everybody attended them. But Ben and I had just fallen in love and we needed time alone. So, whenever we could find an excuse, we would slip away and meet at the lake.

We'd sit on that old wooden dock holding hands and dangling our feet in the water while we gazed at the moon and talked about the future. Sometimes we would kiss for hours and hours. As the summer progressed, we started petting and fondling each other.

At first, Ben just touched my breasts through my top. Then, after a while, I let him unbutton me and reach inside my bra. By mid-August, I was eagerly removing my shirt and bra to let him play with my nipples. It made him hard, and I used to stroke his erection through his pants.

We were tempted to go all the way, but we never did. In fact, we never even took off our pants, except once when we went skinny-dipping in the moonlight. It was the first time I had ever been in the water nude, and it was very exciting. It was also the first time that we saw each other with no clothes on, and that was even more exciting. But for some strange reason, we were careful not to touch each other that night.

Somehow, I managed to keep my virginity until the camp session ended and we all went home. Ben and I continued to see each other in the city and we often talked about our lakeside rendezvouses. We planned to work at the camp again the following summer and fantasized about spending our evenings at the lake. We decided that we would wait until then to go all the way.

I used to make Ben tell me about how it would be. I would make him describe to me in detail what he would do to me and what it would feel like to have intercourse. I guess that was how we started sharing fantasies. To tell you the truth, I think that talking about it was actually more exciting than doing it for the first time.

We never did go back to work at that camp. When we finally did have intercourse, it was in a parking lot in the backseat of a car about a year later. We were so afraid of getting caught that we rushed through it. When it was over, I wasn't even sure it had happened.

We didn't get married for almost three years, but we had sex whenever we could. City life didn't give us many opportunities for romance, though. At a party, for example, we felt lucky if we could sneak into a bathroom together for a quick session. But those fast fucks just didn't satisfy me. Most of the time, I didn't even have an orgasm. So I turned to fantasy to make our sex more romantic. No matter where we were in reality, my mind took us back to the lake at the camp.

At first, I kept the fantasy to myself. I felt too silly to talk about it. It was like a kid's game of make-believe. But it made sex so much better for me that eventually I needed to share it with Ben. So one night on the way to a party I said, "Ben, do you remember those wonderful nights at the lake?"

"Oh, yes," he said with a sigh. "I'll never forget them." I could tell by the expression on his face that the memories were as precious to him as they were to me. "Sometimes," he added, "I think about those nights while we're making love. I even pretend that we're back at camp."

I didn't feel silly anymore. After all, if Ben could admit to his fantasies, I could admit to mine. "Me too," I said. "When I'm standing against a wall with my skirt up around my waist and we're screwing for all we're worth, I remember how peaceful it was by the lake and I imagine that we're there."

At the party later that night, we slipped away for a quick one in one of the bedrooms. I was nervous, afraid that somebody would walk in on us. We both were, I suppose, because we didn't even undress. Ben just unzipped his pants and I lifted my dress. He managed to get inside me by pulling my underwear to one side. I didn't even feel particularly aroused.

Then Ben started to whisper softly. "Remember the night we swam nude in the lake? I'll never forget how excited it made me to see your naked body. Not just your breasts, but everything. I remember my first look at the hair on your pussy. I got so hard that I thought I would come right there. I turned away from you in the water so that my hard-on wouldn't show. But then I turned back again because I wanted to see more of you."

Ben's words made me forget where we were and brought me back to that exciting summer at camp. I was living the fantasy and feeling it. His imagination had merged with mine. I added my own whispered description to his. It felt so natural to be talking about it with him. Before I knew what hit me, I was having a fantastic climax.

Everything changed for us that night. We learned how to use sexual fantasy as a device for heightening our pleasure. No matter where we were and no matter what the circumstances, we could always rely on our imaginations to lift us above our surroundings.

Funny. We've been married for more than twenty years now, and we have as much privacy as we want. But we still use fantasy to add excitement to our life. And the lake at camp is still one of our favorites. That's what I meant when I said that we had been there just a few days ago.

BARBARA AND GARY

Steve:

Barbara has been cutting my hair for the past several years. She loves to talk while she works, and usually manages to carry the conversation without much help from me. When we first met, she talked about everything under the sun. Ever since she learned that Iris and I were writers of erotic fiction, however, her monologues have mainly been about sex.

Recently, Barbara told me that she would like to live in the country as Iris and I do. Although she and her boyfriend, Gary, both love the outdoors, their work schedules keep them inside most of the time. Their only chance to enjoy fresh air and sunshine is when they're out playing golf. "Naturally," Barbara said, "the golf course plays an important part in our sexual fantasies . . ."

* * *

You might say Gary and I are golfing nuts. But I don't think the game intrigues me as much as the setting. I remember the first time Gary took me to the golf course. I was absolutely enthralled by all that lush manicured green. It was like looking at a velvet carpet that seemed to go on forever. It was so calming and peaceful. The blue sky and the warm sun gave my body a feeling of security.

My mind wandered as Gary taught me how to play. I kept imagining what it would be like for Gary and me to have the whole place to ourselves with nobody else around. I pictured us making love on the ground and feeling the grass against our skin. I enjoyed the game, but I wasn't always concentrating on it. Half the time I was having those sexy thoughts.

The following week, when Gary asked if I wanted to play again, I jumped at the chance. As we walked from hole to hole, I looked around for good locations for outdoor sex. By the time we got home, I was so worked up thinking about it that I practically raped Gary. We made it right there on the living-room rug, and I came so fast that Gary was surprised.

"What aphrodisiac have you been taking?" he asked.

So I told him about my golf-course fantasies. And, boy, did he love it. He made me describe my imaginary settings in detail. He had been playing on that course for years, so most of the time he recognized the locations as I described them. We both got so excited that we made love again, only more slowly this time.

When we drove out to the course the next Saturday, Gary said that he would show me some great spots for us to do it. While we were playing, he pointed to clumps of brush or patches of open grass and said, "What about right here? This would be a good place." I got so excited that I couldn't wait for us to get home.

That night while we lay in bed touching and petting each other, our fantasies stimulated us. I closed my eyes and listened while Gary stroked me and whispered in my ear. When he stroked me, he said, "We're lying on that shady spot near the fifth green. The sun is shining on us. And we're all alone."

For me, it felt like we were really there. It's amazing how a fantasy can be part of real life if you let it. My body felt the mattress, but my mind felt cool green blades of grass. We were in our bedroom with the window closed, but I imagined a soft breeze blowing against my naked skin and I could almost smell the fragrance of new-mown lawns.

When Gary climbed on top of me, I pictured a canopy of trees above us. The thought of making love under the sun and the sky intensified the sensation of every thrust. I could tell by the way Gary was moaning that it was special for him too. We came at almost the same time. It was the first time we ever got that close to a simultaneous orgasm.

We play a lot of golf now. We manage to get out almost every week and we go to all different courses. As we play, we keep looking for good locations to fantasize about later. I think we're both dreaming of finding a course someday where we can be totally alone. If that ever happened, we would just strip off our clothes and make it right there on the green. Until then, we'll just have to use our imagination.

HELEN AND COLE

Iris:

When Cole and his first wife were getting their divorce, Steve was Cole's lawyer. Two years later, when he and Helen were married, they invited Steve and me to the wedding. Since then, we have gotten together on a social basis every now and then.

Helen is a sales representative for an office-supplies company, but she thinks of herself as a budding author. She peppers her speech with flowery metaphors and poetic images. For the past two years, she has been writing a novel in her spare time. I ask about it whenever I see her, but she always says that she doesn't want to discuss it until it is finished. Instead, she prefers to hear about the things Steve and I are writing, asking me to tell her about whatever we are working on at the moment.

Recently, I ran into her in a coffee shop and we chatted for a while. I mentioned that we were collecting the erotic fantasies of happy couples for this book and asked whether she and Cole had one to contribute. Helen seemed surprised. "If a couple is really happy," she asked, "why would they have to make up an imaginary life?"

I explained that we were using the word "fantasy" to refer to the secrets that mates share in whispers while making love.

"Oh, you mean pillow talk," Helen said. "Sure, we do that. But I never thought of it as fantasy. All we do is reminisce . . ."

* * *

You know, there isn't enough romance in life. Sometimes it seems that all we live for is to get up, go to work, come home, go to bed, and maybe have a little sex once in a while. But when Cole and I want to get into a really romantic mood, we talk about a wonderful night we had when we made love on a beach in Santorini.

Santorini is one of the Greek islands. We took a vacation there three years ago and arranged to rent a house overlooking the Aegean Sea. We had the whole beach to ourselves, and the first night we were there we decided to go for a moonlight swim.

The air smelled like perfume, and the Mediterranean was only a few degrees cooler than the air. There was a feeling of romance in the atmosphere. There was something so sexy about that night and that setting that I found myself getting aroused for no reason at all. When we finished swimming, I said to Cole, "Let's go back to the house and make love."

Instead of answering, Cole took me in his arms. We just stood there for a moment, pressing our bodies together and kissing. I was already feeling horny, and his hands moving over my wet skin were intensifying the feeling. Before I knew it, Cole unhooked the top of my bathing suit. "Wait," I said. "Wait until we get inside the house." But he pulled the top off me and took me in his arms again.

When my breasts pressed against his chest, I put my arms around him and held him tight. He felt so strong and powerful. I started to run my fingers over his back, marveling at the hardness of his muscles. He was beginning to grind against me, and he was hard down there too. It was exciting to stand there on the beach with my bra off and my nipples drilling little holes in his chest. But I was nervous that someone might see us. "Please," I said. "Let's go inside."

Cole didn't say a word. He just crushed me in his marvelous arms and pressed his lips against mine. Somehow the way he held me made me forget my nervousness for the moment. He was guarding me, protecting me. I felt safe and secure. And his kisses were making me drunk.

We stood in each other's embrace, swaying a little. His hands began stroking my back, moving lower all the time. He kneaded my buttocks gently and then slipped his fingertips inside the bottom of my swimsuit. When I felt him drawing it downward, I got tense again. "No, please. Not out here."

Cole disregarded my words. He just pulled my suit slowly down until I could feel the warm night air caressing my bare bottom. It was a little scary to be doing that on the beach. But very exciting too.

I kept trying to insist that we go inside. But he silenced me with his lips. I tried to step out of his embrace, but his arms held me without effort. I tried to keep my legs together so that my suit wouldn't come off, but he didn't even seem to notice. Before I knew it, the suit was around my ankles. Without even realizing it, I stepped out of it.

The way he held me made it clear that he was going to take me right there and then. But I wasn't nervous anymore. I was thrilled. He was obsessed, possessed. He wanted me so much that nothing was going to stop him. He was determined, and that excited me. I felt powerless in his arms. His strength was so tender that I just wanted to melt.

I could feel the hardness of him pressing against me through his bathing suit. I wanted to reach down and hold him. To take his massive penis in my hand. But I didn't. He was in complete control of me, and I just didn't feel like I could do anything on my own.

I was completely nude outdoors for the first time in my life. It made me feel vulnerable, totally dependent on his strength. He lifted me up and cradled me in his arms, tilting his head to kiss my breasts and belly. I wanted to spread myself open and give myself to his power. I was purring and moaning softly.

Gently, carefully, he laid me down on that incredibly soft sand. I lay there looking up at him as he stripped off his trunks. In the moonlight, his penis looked like a marble column—long and thick and powerful. He dropped to his knees beside me and began running his hands over my body. He cupped my breasts, lifting them up to his hungry lips. He stroked the valley between them and traced a slow deliberate line across my navel to the edge of my pubic hair.

I parted my thighs and arched my back slightly, lifting myself up toward him just as his hand covered my mound. I raised my arms and encircled his neck, drawing him down on top of me. We kissed again, and I could feel the tip of his penis rubbing against my vaginal lips, trying to find its way inside. When we make love, I usually guide it in with my fingers. But this time I just lay there kissing him and letting him do whatever he wanted with me.

His hand moved between us, squeezing my nipples tenderly. Then he reached down and spread my vagina open with his fingers, easing himself inside me with a slow steady thrust. When I felt him entering me, I sighed. This was what I had wanted. I had wanted it from the moment we arrived in Santorini, but I hadn't known it.

He reached under me with both hands now, gripping my buttocks and pulling my pelvis up against him. He was so masterful that I just abandoned myself to his will. He established the tempo, lifting me up to meet him as he drove forward to penetrate me. My wails of pleasure drowned out the crashing of the waves as he thrust into me again and again.

Involuntarily, my legs went around his waist. I wanted to melt into him, to weld my body to his. He seemed to be getting longer and thicker, plunging deeper inside me than ever before. I could feel his tip battering against the mouth of my womb. For a moment, I was afraid to come. Afraid that I would die from the sheer ecstasy of it.

"Oh, yes," I sobbed. "Do it to me. Oh, yes. It feels so good."

Then the sky exploded. I felt his penis throbbing

and swelling as it started to spurt inside me at the exact moment that my climax overtook me. I can remember how intense it felt, but there's no way I can describe it. I felt like we were coming for hours. Sometimes, just when I thought the orgasm was over, it seemed to be starting up again.

Cole stayed hard, and somehow I knew that he wouldn't get soft until I had all I could stand. We rolled around in the sand, moving our bodies together until the sharp waves of pleasure began to mellow. Then we kissed for a long time with him still inside me. Afterward, we rolled onto our backs and lay side by side, naked in the sand, looking up at the moon and stars.

That vacation—that night—was the most sensual time of our lives. Now, when we want to have a really romantic evening, we lie in bed talking about it. I tell Cole how I remember his strength and his tender power. How he overcame all my nervousness and resistance when he took me on the beach. How excited I was when he picked me up and laid me on the sand. What a thrill it was to feel him spreading me open for his penis to enter. He tells me what he was feeling when he pulled my bathing suit off at the water's edge, and how wonderful it felt when he penetrated me in the open air on the beach.

As we talk about it, we both become aroused. But we don't make love right away. We keep talking until he's as hard as he was that night, and I feel as soft and vulnerable. Then he mounts me the way he did on the beach, pulling me up against him with his hands cupping my buttocks. And in our memory we recapture the romance of Santorini.

4
Read Me the Story; Show Me the Pictures

A recently published pornographic novel contains the following description:

> In her mind's tormented eye, she saw the hazy picture of his penis, dripping with ooze and swollen with desire. Slowly, with love and with tenderness, the bulbous purple cockhead approached her slit, kissing lightly against the furry flanges that guarded its erotic opening. Sighing once more, she drew the lips open with her fingers, sliding their tips through the thick coating of slime which sparkled wetly on the inner surfaces. Then almost imperceptibly, she slipped it inside.

In language better suited to its time, a much older work described the same erotic act:

> I slept, but my heart was awake.
> Hark! My beloved is knocking.
> "Open to me, my sister, my love,
>   my dove, my perfect one,
> For my head is wet with dew
>   my locks with the drops of the night."

I arose to open to my beloved,
   and my hands dripped with myrrh,
   my fingers with liquid myrrh,
   upon the handles of the bolt.
I opened to my beloved.

This poetry can be found in the Old Testament's Song of Songs. Some biblical scholars believe that it was written by Solomon, the Hebrew king whose name is synonymous with wisdom, and that the tale of two lovers is actually an allegory about God's love for the children of Israel. Other experts disagree. None can dispute that the description is erotic, however.

The Song of Songs is far from being antiquity's only erotica. Almost 3,500 years ago, the Egyptian Papyrus of Turin graphically illustrated fourteen positions for sexual intercourse. Another papyrus of the same period depicted two gods in an act of homosexual coupling. Ancient Greek frescoes and tapestries often showed the god Priapus with his tremendous erection being mouthed and mounted by troops of beautiful young girls and boys. Sculptures on the walls of ancient temples in India demonstrate every possible position for human copulation. The *Arabian Nights,* now a source of adventure stories like "Sinbad the Sailor" and "The Forty Thieves," was originally a collection of spoken erotic tales handed down from one generation to the next by Arabs, Persians, and Egyptians.

An obsessive fascination with sex was programmed into us to keep us reproducing and to keep our species alive. From the earliest times, it has driven us to read descriptions and to look at pictures or statues of human beings making love. Unlike the Song of Songs, most erotica makes no pretense at allegorical meaning. It is designed for no other reason than to arouse passion, to inflame sexual desire.

For this reason, we were not surprised to find that many of the couples we interviewed use erotic literature or pictures as the starting point for their sexual fantasies. These people begin with what they see in a book or magazine and then allow their imaginations to take over. Humans all over the world have been doing the same thing for thousands of years.

PHIL AND SUSAN

Steve:

Phil is a photographer who specializes in taking pictures of injured people and damaged automobiles for personal-injury lawyers. When I was in law practice, Phil often helped me to prepare cases for trial by photographing the evidence I wanted preserved. During an idle conversation, I asked whether he had ever photographed nudes. Somehow, I could tell by the secret smile playing over his face that he had a story to tell.

"Only once," he answered. "I took a few nude shots of my wife, Susan. That was before we were married. But, afterward, it led to some of the best sex we've ever had . . ."

* * *

We had only been married a few months and I was working as a processor for a pretty well-known photographer. He did all kinds of magazine layouts, including some centerfold stuff. My job was to develop the prints and touch them up according to his specific instructions. Sometimes he'd have me make dozens of copies of the same shot, using various processing techniques to get subtle differences in contrast and coloring. Then, later, he'd pick out the version he liked best.

One day I found myself working on some shots he had taken of a nude model. She was really good-looking, with the kind of soft round curves that have always appealed to me. Maybe it was unprofessional of me, but I found myself becoming really aroused as I worked with those pictures. I was alone in the darkroom, but still, I felt kind of embarrassed about it. I also felt a little guilty, because I was practically a newlywed. But even though I was getting excited looking at the model, I was thinking about my wife, too, in a way. Then I got this crazy idea.

I had the negative of a head-and-shoulders portrait I had done of Susan. So I put my artistic skills to work combining parts of the two pictures. When I was finished, I had a picture of the nude model's body with Susan's face. It was a pretty good job.

That night, I brought the picture home and showed it to Susan. I told her that it was one of the nudes I had taken of her just before we were married. At first, she just glanced at the photo and she believed me. But when she took a closer look, she said, "Hey, that's not me."

"What are you talking about?" I asked. "Certainly that's you. Look at the face."

"Oh, no it isn't," she said. "My breasts aren't that big. And my nipples aren't that dark."

"Of course they are," I insisted.

Snatching the photo out of my hand, she walked over to the bedroom mirror. She stripped her nightgown off over her head, looking at her reflection and then back at the picture. I could see that she was comparing her own breasts to those of the girl in the photo. "This isn't me," she said. "My nipples definitely aren't that dark."

I came up behind her and reached around to start playing with her breasts. "You may not realize it," I said, "but your nipples always get darker when you get excited. Look in the mirror and you'll see."

For a while, she just stood there watching in the mirror as I rolled her nipples in my fingers to make them really hard.

"Maybe you're right," she said, glancing from the mirror to the picture and back again. But I could tell that she had figured it out. Now she was just playing with me. "Do I really look like that down there, too?" she asked. She rubbed her mound in front of the mirror to make her pussy pout the way the model's did in the picture. I started rubbing it too, and pretty soon we were rolling around on the bed with the picture beside us, having some of the hottest sex we had ever known.

After that, she kept the picture in a drawer of her night table for quite a while. Whenever she felt especially playful, I'd find it on my pillow when we went to bed as a kind of signal. Then we'd have a good time comparing her parts to the picture again.

We still have that picture around somewhere. You know how it is, though. After a while, we got tired of it. But we still play the same game occasionally. Now what I do is get a copy of *Playboy* or *Penthouse* and find a picture in it that really turns me on. Then I just paste a shot of Susan's face over the model's. Usually, I do this without Susan knowing. Then I leave the magazine on our bed.

That night when we're in bed together, nude, Susan will leaf through the magazine until she finds the doctored picture. She'll point at it and say, "Isn't that a good picture of me?"

If it's a picture that emphasizes the model's breasts, she'll say something like "Doesn't that shot make my breasts look big and round? Would you like to feel yourself between them?" Then, while I'm looking at the picture, she'll lie against me pressing her tits against my cock and balls. When she does that, I imagine that it's the woman in the picture. Susan doesn't mind at all. In fact, she gets off on that idea too.

If it happens to be one of those split beaver pictures that show a model with her legs open wide and her pussy all exposed, my wife will imitate the pose right there on the bed. She'll lean back and spread her thighs as far as they can go, stroking herself while I watch. "That's how I posed when we shot that one," she'll say.

Sometimes she takes my hand and puts it on her while I'm looking at the picture in the centerfold. Then, while I stroke her, she describes the way it feels. Or she'll point to places on the picture and say, "Touch me right here," or "Put your tongue on this spot." Then, as I'm doing it to her, I glance at the picture and kind of pretend that I'm doing it to the model.

Sometimes when we make love she leaves the magazine open beside her on the bed. Then, when I climb on top of her, I can look at the photo and get the sensation of making it with the model. Susan knows I'm doing this and doesn't object. She even encourages it.

Once I found a really sexy picture of a model with gorgeous, long blond hair and a brunette pubic bush. When I pasted Susan's face onto the picture, I was careful to leave that blond hair showing. Susan, who is a brunette, thought that the model's body was just like hers. When she looked at the photo, she said, "I had to wear a blond wig for that one. But they couldn't find a wig for down there." That picture seemed to turn her on more than any of the others. And we had a really hot night.

A few days later, Susan surprised me. As I was getting ready for bed, I found the magazine on my pillow, open to that same centerfold. A few moments later, my wife came out of the bathroom wearing a long blond wig. She really got into pretending to be that girl in the picture. For me, it was like making love to a different woman.

She still brings out that picture once in a while and wears that blond wig to bed. It's a way of bringing variety into our marriage and keeping our sex life fresh and spicy. It turns Susan on to imagine that

I'm screwing someone else, as long as it's really her that I'm with. And I must admit, it turns me on, too.

ROSE AND BILL

Iris:

Rose teaches English and American literature at a junior college in Southern California. I first met her when Steve and I were visiting her school to attend a career seminar. After a brief conversation, we discovered that we came from the same neighborhood in New York City and that we had lived only a few blocks from each other when we were growing up. Although we did not know each other then, we found that we had some acquaintances in common. Before long, we became rather friendly.

Probably Rose's most impressive characteristic is her air of sophistication. Without seeming arrogant or superior, she gives the impression of having done and seen everything. For that reason, I was a little surprised at the way she reacted when I told her that Steve and I were working on a book about sexual fantasy.

Rose giggled. "I didn't know there was any such thing as sexual fantasy," she said, "until a year after I was married. And then I had to learn it from John Cleland."

For a moment, Rose remembered that she was a literature teacher. "He wrote *Fanny Hill*, you know. Around 1740. I owe an awful lot to Cleland.

His book taught me to fantasize. If it wasn't for that, I don't think Bill and I would be very happy today . . .''

* * *

Bill and I got married the week after we graduated from high school. We were both kind of ignorant about sex. We had necked at parties like all the other kids in our crowd, but we never really went beyond deep kissing. On a couple of occasions, I let Bill touch my breasts through my sweater, but we never went further than that.

On our wedding night, I was so nervous about having intercourse that I didn't believe I would be able to go through with it. I insisted on getting undressed in the bathroom because I couldn't stand the idea of letting anyone—including my new husband—see me naked. Bill didn't even object.

The truth is that he didn't know much more about sex than I did. Once, in his senior year, his older brother had set him up with a prostitute. But he didn't learn much from her. Apparently, neither of them took their clothes off. All she did was open his pants, lift her skirt, and let him stick it in her. It was over before it began.

Well, that's the way it was for me that first time. When I came out of the bathroom wearing my long flannel nightgown, Bill was already in bed. I made him shut the light before I got in beside him. He was so excited that his hands were shaking. He climbed on top of me and fumbled around for a while, trying to get himself into my vagina. I don't even think he touched me with his hands. Finally, he found my opening and shoved his penis all the way in. At the same time, he started making grunting sounds. I never even had a chance to feel the pain when he broke my hymen. There was no time. He started to come immediately. Then he slipped out and rolled over beside me.

That's how it went for almost a year. Two or three times a week, he would jump on, pant and puff for a while, and then jump off, satisfied. Don't get me wrong. I didn't mind. Nobody ever told me any different, so I figured that was how it was supposed to be. Boys had always seemed to be preoccupied with sex while girls were more interested in romance. It seemed perfectly proper for me to lie under him for a moment or two while he got whatever it was that he got out of it.

I suppose I felt a vague sense of dissatisfaction. But, I didn't really know what I was dissatisfied about. And I didn't really think there was anything I could or should do about it.

Then, about a year after we were married, I happened to be browsing through some old books at a rummage sale when I came across one called *Fanny Hill: Memoirs of a Woman of Pleasure*. The name sounded awfully familiar, although I couldn't remember where I'd heard of it before. The book was only a dime, so I bought it along with a few others. When I got home, it suddenly came to me. Back in high school, I had heard some of the girls giggling and whispering about *Fanny Hill*. It was supposed to be very sexy.

Bill was at work, and I really didn't have anything much to do, so I sat down and started reading it. What a shock! Fanny, the girl telling the story, started having erotic adventures almost from the first page. My ears burned as I read about her sex experiences, first with other girls and then with men she hardly knew. I'm sure I was shaking my head in the horror of disapproval, when suddenly I found my reactions changing.

I had come to a scene in which Fanny was seated on a couch beside a young man. She described in detail how he lifted her petticoats and removed her undergarments to stare openly at what she called her ''region of delight'' and at all the ''luxurious landscape 'round it''. The thought of her genitals exposed to his hungry gaze made me feel kind of warm.

I continued reading her description of the way he opened her folding lips with his fingers and of the secret places where he kissed her. His touch and his examination, she said, made a certain tiny part of her grow stiff. As I read it, my vulva started to itch, and I just had to rub it. I did so unconsciously at first, reading on with a vague sense of guilt.

Before I knew what was happening, my vagina was on fire and a tiny part of me was growing stiff, too. Putting the book down beside me, I lifted my skirt and pulled down my panties to take a good look. I think it was the first time I ever got more than a fleeting glance of my own sex organs. It was exciting. I could see the pink swollen button that Fanny referred to in her narrative. I had never even known it existed before.

Hungry for knowledge, I returned to Fanny's words, staring down at myself time and again to confirm her descriptions. She referred to her vagina as a deep flesh wound, and when I looked at mine, I saw exactly that. She compared her puckering sex to a hungry mouth with inflamed, swollen lips surrounded by a beard of ringlets. Looking at my own naked femininity, I found that her words described it perfectly.

I lay back on the couch and read on. Now, as Fanny detailed the things her young companion did to her, I could picture them in my mind. I shuddered with curiosity as his lips grazed over her pouting orifice. I imagined the clammy moisture that coated his mouth after he kissed her fragrant opening. And then a strange thing occurred.

Instead of seeing these things happening to Fanny, I began to see them happening to myself. I read on for a while, picturing the young man's tongue on my sex, imagining his fingers petting my vulva. Then I lay the book aside and closed my eyes. I saw his tongue entering my slit. But not with Bill's brutal swiftness. This was tender and slow and thorough.

Without realizing it, I had placed my hands on my groin and was running my fingers through my curling pubic hair. Then, for the first time in my life, I began masturbating. I didn't think about it at all. I just did it. By instinct. Within seconds, I was having my first orgasm. All the while, my mind was reeling with mixed images of Fanny Hill and myself.

Afterward, I was worried and confused. I realized how incomplete my sex life had been. I wondered about my marriage to Bill and how it could possibly continue. Then I decided I would have to make Bill discover what I had just discovered.

By the time he got home from work, I had it figured out. I was dressed in a full skirt with petticoats like those I imagined Fanny was wearing. I didn't have any panties on. When Bill walked in, he kissed me as usual and asked me what was for dinner. But I led him to the couch and made him sit next to me.

"Wait for dinner," I said. "I want to read you something."

Without any explanation, I began reading him the chapter that had so dazzled me that afternoon. He was confused at first, not really listening. Then a word or two struck him and he began paying attention. When I got to the part where the young man lifted Fanny's petticoats, I threw back my own, wantonly displaying my moist genitals to Bill.

Bill was surprised. But I've got to give him credit for being a quick learner. Within minutes, he was kneeling on the floor between my thighs staring at my pouting sex and petting it with his hands. By the time Fanny described how stiff and inflamed that tiny part of her was becoming, Bill had discovered my clitoris and was playing with it, first with his fingers, then with his mouth. I tried to read on, but my eyes started to blur and I had to close them.

Moments later I had the second orgasm of my life. It was even better than the first. I moaned and sobbed uncontrollably. As it wound down, I found myself feeling a little guilty for taking so much and not giving anything in return. But when I looked into Bill's face, I saw a sparkle in his eyes that had never been there before. He was proud to have given me such intense pleasure. He kissed me with a depth that made me know that our marriage would be getting better and better from that point on. And it has.

Now our sex life is wonderfully varied. Even now, though, when I want something really special, I make Bill sit next to me on the couch while I read to him. Sometimes I read passages from *Lady Chatterley's Lover* or some other classic work of erotic fiction. Sometimes I read that same passage from Cleland's *Fanny Hill*.

While I'm reading, Bill and I imagine the characters in the story until, after a while, we begin imagining ourselves in the story. Then the fun begins again. We may start by doing whatever it is I'm reading about. But eventually we begin to elaborate until we're creating our own fantasies and acting them out with all the passion of that first time.

STAN AND MICHELLE

Steve:

After one of my lectures on sex and the law, Stan, a mental-health nurse, approached me with a few questions. He was particularly interested in knowing whether a husband and wife could be prosecuted for taking obscene photographs of each other. I explained that the United States Supreme Court has created a very specific definition for ''obscenity,'' and that the term cannot be applied to photographs just because they are erotic.

Stan, a very chatty fellow, started describing the photos without any embarrassment whatsoever. When he finished, I assured him that what he and his wife were doing was perfectly legal. Then I got his permission to include an account of it in this book.

* * *

When Michelle and I were dating, we enjoyed having sexy conversations over the telephone. We had been going together for a while and often spent our evenings making love. Sometimes during the day, I'd call her at work and talk about the things we had done the previous night. Or she'd call me and describe the things we were going to do the next time we saw each other. We kept it up after we got married. Then, quite by accident, we discovered a way to give our fantasy conversations a new twist.

I had just bought one of those instant cameras—the kind that give you a picture within a few seconds after you shoot it. This one was pretty sophisticated. I was sitting in bed reading the instructions and trying to figure out how to use it when Michelle went to get something out of her dresser. She was wearing a short nightgown, and when she bent over to reach into the drawer, her bare ass was facing me. I couldn't resist taking a picture of her in that position.

I was going to show it to Michelle, but the phone rang, and I got distracted and somehow didn't get around to it. The next morning, by the time I remembered the photo, Michelle had already gone to work. So I stuck it in my pocket as I was leaving the house. That afternoon, I was having lunch by myself when I remembered the picture and took it out to look at it.

It was very sexy. Michelle's body always excites

me, with or without clothes. But this picture was special. The brief nightgown formed a kind of frame around the firm cheeks of her backside with the dark shadow between them. And I could just about see some of her hair peeking through from the other side. As I looked at it, I found myself getting all turned on.

I dialed the number of Michelle's office. When I got her on the phone, I said, "You'll never guess what I'm looking at."

"What?" she asked.

"The nicest bare ass in town," I answered. Then I told her about the photo. I described the way she looked in it and how excited it was making me.

Michelle fell right into the game. "Tonight," she said, "I'll show it to you again. I'll even let you kiss it if you want."

We talked that way for a while and then we both went back to work. But it was hard for me to concentrate. By the time I got home, my head was full of sex ideas.

We rushed to the bedroom immediately. As we undressed, we took turns photographing each other with the new camera. After we were nude, we modeled for each other in the sexiest poses we could think of. We went through three or four film cartridges until we were so excited that we jumped into the bed and started making love. I think we must have had about four orgasms each that night.

The next day, Michelle called me at work. She was looking at some of the photographs we had taken the night before. In whispers, she described each of them in detail, turning me on all over again. She talked about how she looked in the ones I had taken, and told me how hot she was getting looking at the ones she had taken of me. A few hours later, she called me again and got me even hotter. That night we had some magnificent sex.

We've been doing it ever since. We still have that first set of pictures. By now, of course, we've added lots of others to the collection. I recently got a tripod for the camera so that now we can even set it up to take shots of the two of us together.

We love to call each other on the phone during the day and fantasize together about our sex life. Looking at the pictures while we talk about it makes the fantasies more real. It's almost like having real live sex in the middle of the workday, but over the phone. And we can always count on it whipping us up to a night of sexual delight.

5 What If We Get Caught

In 1947, British physician Eustace Chesser wrote that "Fear plays havoc with the sex lives of tens of thousands of people." More than forty years later, it is obvious that fear continues to play a major role in influencing sexual behavior. Although we may become fearful or anxious about any of the things that are important to us, sexual fears hold a very special place in Western thought. Some writers blame this on the attitudes of medieval Christianity.

During the Middle Ages, sexually promiscuous men were sometimes punished by castration. Immoral women were dragged through the streets, publicly tortured, and stoned to death. People who spoke against sexual repression could be convicted of heresy and killed.

Literature of the period is filled with examples of this antisex philosophy. *The Decameron,* written by Giovanni Boccaccio about 1350, contains dozens of stories in which men and women are punished severely for yielding to their lustful desires. In one of these tales, King Frederick of Sicily finds two lovers sleeping together in a room of his palace. Incensed by this discovery, Frederick orders their immediate execution. The unfortunate pair are brought naked to the town square, where they are tied back-to-back to a stake and prepared for burning. As firewood is being piled around them, the lovers beg to be bound face-to-face so that the last thing each of them sees will be the other. Luckily, an admiral of the royal fleet is so impressed by their sentiment that he arranges to set them free.

Today, no one is put to death for having sex with a consenting adult partner. But although the risks are not as serious as they were in the fourteenth century, the feelings of shame we harbor about our sexual conduct make the danger of discovery very real. For example, the expression "caught with his pants down" uses an obviously sexual image to describe any painfully embarrassing situation, even if sex isn't involved at all.

For many people, this sense of sexual shame is like a burning at the emotional stake. The possibility of strangers walking in on them while they are having sex is a potent source of anxiety that drives all feelings of desire from their libidos. For others, however, this emotion adds so much spice to their lovemaking that they deliberately try to evoke feelings of fear in their intimate moments.

Many of the couples to whom we spoke told us that while making love they enjoy imagining that they are in danger of being caught. A few of them increase the pleasure of these fantasies by actively creating a possibility of discovery. Although all admitted frankly that real or imagined fear makes their sex play more arousing, none offered an explanation for this reaction.

Psychologists disagree about why fear increases sexual excitement in some individuals. All agree about the physical results, however. The sympathetic nervous system responds to fear by causing increases in adrenaline production, heart rate, blood sugar, respiration, and in the supply of blood to external muscles. Maybe it's just a coincidence and maybe it isn't, but these physical reactions are almost always associated with sexual arousal.

ABBI AND BARRY

Steve:

When I was in law practice, Barry, an older attorney, had an office in the same building as mine. I always considered Barry the most conservative man I knew. His suits and ties were always of an identical solid color—brown, black, gray, or blue. All his shirts were white with starch in the collars. Barry was an office lawyer who never appeared in court. Every morning at precisely 8:55, he sat down at his uncluttered desk. There, wearing a serious expression, he worked until 12:15, when he went out to eat lunch—always at the same restaurant—returning to his desk no later than 1:35.

His wife, Abbi, on the other hand, was flamboyant in dress and behavior. She was fond of wearing bright colors and styled her hair like a teenager's. She had a contagious, musical laugh with which she punctuated almost every sentence. Whenever I saw her with Barry, I found myself wondering what they could possibly have in common. Then a conversation between Abbi and me reminded me of how foolish it can be to form conclusions about people based only on their outward appearances.

One night on the way out of the office, I saw Abbi and Barry sitting in their car in our building's underground parking lot. According to Barry's usual schedule, he should have left half an hour earlier, so I thought that they might be having car trouble. When I stopped to ask if everything was all right, I noticed that Abbi was wearing a fur coat. I thought it strange for the season, but attributed it to Abbi's flair. After they assured me that they were just talking and that their car was fine, I went on my way.

About a week later, Abbi came for Barry a bit early and found him tied up on the phone. While waiting for him, she dropped into my office and we chatted idly for a few moments. Then, with an impish smile, she said, "Last week when you saw us in the parking lot, I'll bet it never occurred to you that I had nothing on under my coat."

Startled, I said, "No, it sure didn't. But I'd love to hear about it."

Abbi giggled. "I kind of thought you would . . ."

* * *

You know, everybody thinks my Barry is a teddy bear, but sexually he's a tiger. God, I remember when we first started dating, just after he finished law school. Wherever we went—movie, dinner, whatever—he could never keep his hands off me. He'd stroke my leg under the table or feel me up in a dark theater. Best of all were the times in his car.

We'd look for some quiet place to park. Sometimes we drove around for hours trying to find the perfect location. Then we'd climb into the backseat and really get it on. You wouldn't believe the positions we managed to get into in that car.

Of course, no matter how carefully we selected the parking spot, there was always some danger that we would be seen. In a way, that sense of danger made our romantic interludes even more exciting. The possibility of getting caught was always in the back of our minds. In the beginning, we hurried through our lovemaking because of it. But after a while, we would deliberately prolong our sessions, savoring the risk.

We still have great sex, but I guess I miss the excitement of those days. So last week I thought I'd liven things up a bit. I had dropped Barry off in the morning, planning to pick him up after work. Just before I came by, I called him to say that I didn't want to come up to the office because I really wasn't dressed. He agreed to meet me downstairs in the parking lot.

He didn't know it, of course, but I meant it literally. I showered and perfumed myself, but I didn't put on a stitch of clothing except for my fur coat. When I walked out of the house that way, I was already aroused. As I slid into the car, my coat opened, revealing my bare legs almost up to my naked crotch. I know that nobody saw me, but it felt delicious to think that somebody could have.

In the parking lot, I waited for Barry, imagining his reaction. I remained behind the wheel until he got in beside me. Then, as I leaned over to kiss him hello, I let the coat fall open.

He was shocked. "My God, Abbi," he said. "Where are your clothes?"

Now I opened the coat all the way. "I told you I wasn't dressed," I said.

Barry just sat there staring at me. I could see that he was getting aroused, though. Suddenly, he put his arms around me and kissed me with passion.

"I was thinking about the old days," I said. "When we used to take off our clothes and make it in the car. I was thinking about doing it again that way."

At this point, Barry got nervous and began tugging my coat closed. A good thing, too, because you came by just a few minutes later. After you left, Barry said, "That was a close one." But I could see that he was remembering the way the risk of getting caught had spiced up our courtship.

"You know we're not kids anymore," I said. "And we're married. We wouldn't really get into any trouble if we were seen."

"But think of how embarrassing it would be in our present position," Barry replied.

"Only if we get caught," I answered, opening the coat again. "It would be so easy. You could unzip your pants and I could sit on your lap with the coat covering us. Even if somebody came by, they wouldn't know what we were doing. They'd just think we were acting silly."

I knew that we wouldn't really do it, but I could see that Barry was enjoying the idea. His hands were caressing me under my coat as I spoke, encouraging me to go on.

"Or I could bend over and take you in my mouth," I added.

"Tell you what," Barry said. "Let's change seats, and you can tell me all about it while I drive us home." His voice was hoarse with excitement.

I got out and walked around the car while he slid into the driver's seat. When I was directly in front of the car, I turned to face him and held my coat wide open, giving him a complete view of my nakedness through the windshield. Then I closed it again and got in on the passenger's side.

As Barry drove out of the parking lot, I talked about some of the times we had done it in the car when we were younger. I reminded him about a dinner date we had one night while he was studying for the bar exam. It had been more than a week since we saw each other, and I was so horny that when I got dressed for our date, I didn't put on any underwear. Just before we got out of the car to go into the restaurant, I took his hand and placed it under my skirt. He was so surprised to feel me when he was expecting to feel panties that he was too excited to eat. Instead of ordering dinner, he told the waiter that we had changed our minds and insisted on leaving. We drove about two blocks and parked on a quiet residential street where we made love from start to finish in about thirty seconds.

I could tell that my talking about it was getting to Barry. Although he usually concentrates on his driving when he's behind the wheel, he kept taking his eyes off the road to glance at me while I spoke.

Whenever we stopped at a light, I deliberately opened my coat to let him see the parts of me that are usually covered in public. Once I thought I noticed a truck driver watching, and this brought back the excitement that comes with the possibility of being caught. I think Barry noticed it too.

I continued describing sexy experiences from our past until Barry was beside himself with excitement. "I hope we don't run into traffic, tonight of all nights," he gasped. "I can't wait to get you home."

"I don't know," I answered. "If traffic gets bad enough to come to a standstill, we can just crawl into the backseat and do it while we wait for the cars to get moving again." Then I started to describe how it would feel to make love with all the people in the cars and trucks around us watching every detail. I must admit the conversation was arousing me too.

By the time we got home, we were both ravenous with lust. Of course, I'm not planning to tell you any of the details of what came after. But I assure you that you young guys could learn a lot from my Barry. He was so aroused by my little fantasy game that he could have put men twenty years his junior to shame.

When we made love the next night and the night after that, Barry kept talking about my naked visit to the parking lot. He even asked me to walk around the bedroom wearing nothing but my fur coat. I think he's actually considering the possibility of getting it on in the car like I suggested.

I hope we both work up the nerve to do it like that someday, but for now our fantasy will just have to do. And, by the way, I know what you're thinking. If we ever get around to doing it in the car, I have no intention of telling you when or where.

MERILEE AND JACK

Iris:

When Steve and I first settled in Southern California, we kept a few milk goats in our yard as a hobby. Since we didn't own a male goat, we had to bring our females to a nearby farm for breeding. Jack and Merilee, the owners of the farm, were known throughout the vicinity as the Goat People.

Jack was a dour man in bib-top overalls. He was in his forties, but his expression made him look a bit older. I visited the farm several times, but never heard him speak more than fifteen words. Merilee, on the other hand, was a pleasant woman who loved to chat. On more than one occasion, she surprised me with the candor of her conversation and with the frankness of the language she used when talking about her goats, their parts, and their breeding.

One afternoon, while she and I were standing outside her barn waiting for her buck goat to become interested in my doe, Merilee surprised me by saying, "You're the folks that write the dirty books, aren't you?"

Although Steve and I didn't make a secret of our occupation, I hadn't thought that the Goat Lady knew anything about us. I was silent for a moment, trying to frame a response, but all I could think of saying was "Well, I wouldn't call them that, exactly."

"Oh, I didn't mean no offense," Merilee said apologetically. "I just meant that you write books about sex. Isn't that right?"

I was becoming embarrassed, and it must have shown, because she immediately added, "There's nothing wrong with books about sex. I kind of like them. In fact, I got a story that I always thought would go good in a dirty book. Maybe you can use it. Only don't mention our names. It's about Jack and me. And this here barn." She pointed her chin toward the wooden building before us. "Jack and me did it in this barn before we even owned the place . . ."

* * *

We're from the Midwest, originally. But six years ago, when a developer bought the land I inherited from my folks, we decided to move to California, where the winters wouldn't be so cold. Jack came out by himself to look around while I stayed home to get things in order. After two weeks, he called me up, all excited. He said he had found the place of our dreams and told me to fly down immediately.

Jack was so eager to show me this farm that he had the real-estate broker with him when he met me at the airport. We put my valise in the trunk of the broker's car, and she drove straight out here. I wanted to see the house first, but all Jack could talk about was the barn. So the broker told us to go ahead and look it over while she waited for us up at the house.

Jack took my hand and led me to the barn. We

walked around the outside for a little while. I was wearing a long dress and I had to keep lifting it up so's it wouldn't drag in the dirt as we crept through the fences. Every time I did, Jack kind of stared at my legs with a hungry look in his eyes. I still remember that it made me feel glamorous to have him look at me that way. After a while, he said he wanted to go inside so I could see the stock stalls.

It was kind of dark and cool in the barn, the way a barn ought to be on a hot day like this. I was turning my head, trying to get my eyes adjusted to the dark, when Jack suddenly grabbed me from behind. You know, Jack don't say much, but he's a very passionate man. We hadn't seen each other for more than two weeks, and that's the longest we'd ever been apart.

He started touching and feeling me all over, and I was really getting worked up. I said, "Don't, Jack. What if somebody sees us?" But he just stuck his hands under my skirt and started rubbing my spot with his fingers. I could feel my cotton underpants getting all wet, and I knew I really didn't want him to stop. A second later, he had my dress up around my waist and he was pushing himself against me.

"What if the real-estate lady walks in, Jack?" I said. But Jack acted like he hadn't heard me.

I've always tried to act proper, but I'll admit I didn't put up too much of a struggle that time. The truth was, the idea that the real-estate agent might walk in on us was making the whole thing kind of exciting. In fact, I think I even wanted her to catch us.

Jack was so horny, he didn't even try to get my

underpants off. Just sort of pulled them to one side and shoved himself against me. His jeans were open and his pecker stabbed at me, trying to find its way in. I remember closing my eyes and imagining that woman watching us from the doorway the way I sometimes watch the goats doing it. I was thinking of us as a couple of rutting animals, and it was really making me hot.

Jack's a very considerate lover. Usually when we do it, he's real controlled and holds himself for a long time so's I don't miss mine. But that day he was like a buck goat. All he wanted was to get it into me and start screwing. I could feel his need. He was out of control. And I was starting to get that way too.

He humped at me again and again, bumping himself against my tender place and making me as horny as he was. I guess I kind of put one foot up on a rail to make it a little easier for him. That seemed to drive him nuts. A second later, he was in me. Oh, God, it was good. I felt wanton, if you know what I mean. Like we were doing something really nasty, but oh so nice. All the while, I pictured the real-estate lady walking in on us and watching.

We rocked hard against each other. Jack was really in heat; I guess we both were. Didn't take more than a couple of seconds for him to start to bellow. I knew he was gettin' off. Then, before I knew it, I was hollerin' and gettin' off too. I was kind of hoping that even if nobody saw us, at least somebody would hear us.

Man, we were quick. I think the risk of getting caught had a lot to do with that. Afterward, Jack kissed me in a funny kind of way and then zipped himself up while I got my panties untwisted.

After a while, he looked around the barn and said, "I just know this place is going to bring us good luck."

We went right back to the house and made an offer on the farm. And we have never regretted it.

And I'll tell you something else: we never forgot that first time we did it out here in the barn. Even now, sometimes when I'm milking the goats, Jack'll come up in back of me and touch my behind. He says, "Hey, Merry, you remember that day when we came here with the real-estate agent?"

The minute I hear him say it, I get all wet and ready. Sometimes he teases me about it for a while, saying, "You know, whenever I see her in town, she looks at me kind of funny. I have a feeling she sneaked on over here and watched us that time." He'll make a remark like that every couple of minutes until I'm dying to have him give it to me that same way again right here.

Sometimes, I just lift my skirts and we do it in the barn again like we did it that day—standing up, without even getting undressed. Other times, we talk about it all day long, until bedtime. Then, when we get into bed, he does it to me real slow while he talks about it. I love to pretend that someone did catch us in the act, that someone we see all the time now was actually watching while I lifted my foot up onto the rail and Jack slipped it into me. It always makes me horny, and no matter how tired I am, it always gives me the energy for a night of hot sex.

TONY AND VICKI

Iris:

Tony is a friend who studied architecture but decided that he preferred constructing buildings to designing them. About a year ago, he got a contractor's license. Since then, he has been trying to establish himself in the construction business. Recently, I put him in touch with an acquaintance who was renovating an apartment building and was looking for a contractor to handle the construction work. A few days afterward, Tony dropped in to see me, wearing his usual cocky smile. "I got the job," he boasted. "Mainly because I'm the right contractor for it. But I must admit, I wouldn't have gotten it without your referral. So I'm going to do you a real favor in return."

I couldn't imagine what he had in mind, so I just raised an eyebrow.

Tony took on the attitude of a king bestowing a prized gift. "I've heard about that book you and your husband are writing," he said. "And I'm going to give you permission to use one of my very own fantasies in it."

Laughing, I said, "I'm underwhelmed. What makes you think we would want a fantasy of yours?"

"Because it's a great one," Tony said. "My wife, Vicki, loves it, and I'm sure that when you hear it, you'll love it too . . ."

* * *

It all started when I was in college. I was always broke in those days, living from one financial-aid check to the next. I only had a couple of pairs of jeans and a few shirts to my name. Most of the time, I couldn't even afford to buy underwear or socks.

When I went to the laundromat, it took all the clothes I owned to make up a full load. I would go at three or four in the morning, when nobody else was around, and take off whatever I was wearing to throw in the washer with the rest of my stuff. I was worried that a cop would come in and arrest me for indecent exposure, so I used to borrow a towel from my roommate to wrap myself in while waiting for the wash to be done.

I've always had nice memories of those late-night visits to the laundromat. I'd just sit there covered by the towel, reading magazines. I used to imagine what would happen if some woman came in and found me that way.

In my fantasy, she was a beautiful woman who didn't know me at all. When she first noticed me, she would be shocked. But this would change immediately to fascination. Without a word, she would put a quarter in the dryer and flip the lever to HOT. Then she would get completely undressed and walk toward me. She would pull me out of my chair and remove my towel so I'd be standing there naked with my dick as hard as a rock.

Taking hold of it, she'd lead me to the dryer. She'd lift her naked body and perch on its hot surface. Spreading her legs, she'd show me how puffy and wet she was. As I'd move toward her, her legs would wrap around me and she'd guide me into her.

Sometimes I got so into that fantasy that I'd stand by the hot dryer and reach under the towel. There was something really exciting about jerking off there in the laundromat. Any minute, someone could come in and catch me. It was just like in the fantasy, where someone might walk in and find us screwing. It got so that I began to look forward to doing the wash.

It's a good thing I met Vicki soon afterward, or I think I might have become some kind of laundromat pervert. Vicki and I started living together almost immediately. We were both students, so we shared all the household tasks, and that meant going to the laundromat together. Usually, we did this between classes in the middle of the afternoon. But one day I was feeling sexy and got a brainstorm.

When Vicki said she wanted to go do the laundry, I found an excuse to put it off until after dinner. Then I stalled some more. Finally, at about one in the morning, I said, "Okay, let's go do the wash."

Vicki looked at me like I was crazy, but didn't object.

It was a rainy night, so we had the place completely to ourselves. As we put our stuff into the washer, I peeled off my clothes and said, "Hey, nobody's around. Let's wash everything. Like I used to do before I met you."

Vicki was startled by my suggestion. "Aren't you afraid someone will come in and see you like that?" she asked.

"I never got caught before," I said. "And look at that rain. Nobody in their right mind is going to come out on a night like this to do laundry."

As I spoke, I started undressing her, tossing her clothing into the wash. She whispered, "No," a few times, but I guess I must have convinced her, because she didn't make any real effort to stop me. When we were both naked, I started the washer.

"Let's move toward the back," Vicki said nervously. "So that no one can see us from outside."

That suited me just fine, because that's where the dryers were. I led her up to one of them and started it up, selecting the hottest setting. We stood there kissing for a few minutes until the dryer had really warmed up. Then I lifted Vicki and sat her on top of it. For a moment, she wriggled her hips around in a little circle, pressing herself against the warm metal. I could see from the expression on her face that the heat of the machine against her membranes was exciting her.

Although I had never told her about my laundromat fantasy, she seemed to move her legs in exactly the same way as my imaginary lady. As I drove into her, Vicki kept saying "Oh, God, I hope nobody comes in now. Oh, what if somebody sees us?"

The weather conditions made it pretty safe, but of course there was still some possibility of someone walking in on us. For both of us, it was a very exciting possibility. It made us just nervous enough to delay our climaxes, and that was very exciting too. By the time we were finished, the wash was done.

We've talked about that experience many times since then, even though we never did it quite like that again. Some nights when we're in bed, one of us brings it up, describing the mixture of fear and excitement we felt. Talking about it gets us both steaming hot and always leads us on to terrific sex.

Now that we have a house, we even reenact it sometimes in our own laundry room. Occasionally, when we're feeling especially horny, we do the laundry late at night. Then we reminisce about that laundromat scene as we take off our clothes and throw them into the wash. Vicki sits naked on the dryer and I stand in front of her. We make love with the washer and dryer running, taking turns whispering our own versions of the memory. Of course, nobody can walk in on us, but it's fun to imagine that someone might.

Oh, I've gotten myself all excited just telling you about it. I think I'm going to run home and help Vicki with the wash.

Didn't I tell you you were going to love it?

6

What Did You Say Your Name Was?

In Erica Jong's uninhibited novel, *Fear of Flying*, the narrator discusses one of her favorite fantasies—the Zipless Fuck. What makes it "zipless" is a passion so intense that zippers fall away and undergarments blow off. She says that in the ultimate zipless fuck, brevity and anonymity are elements of this passion. The participants must have sex as soon as they meet and must part immediately afterward without ever learning each other's name.

In one of the book's zipless-fuck scenarios, an unshaven soldier takes a seat next to a widow wearing a black dress in a railroad compartment while traveling through the Italian countryside. Silently he strokes her thighs. Moments later, as the train passes through a tunnel, the soldier and the widow have intercourse without speaking a word to each other. At the next station, the widow gets off the train.

Ordinarily, the sex act is associated with emotion and commitment—often a lifetime commitment. For many people, however, lifetime commitments seem to be prisons from which there can be no escape. This can introduce an element of insecurity or fear into sexuality. Most of the time, this fear is directed not at the physical sex act itself, but at the difficulties that are always likely to accompany an emotional relationship. As a result, many people attempt to separate the physical aspects of sex from the emotional ones. The end result of this separation is the zipless fuck.

This may explain why some men deal with prostitutes, although less impersonal sex is available to them without charge. Xaviera Hollander, the Happy Hooker, describes men of this type in one of her books. She says that they are willing to risk VD, robbery, and physical assault for the "special kick" of picking up a streetwalker and having sex with her behind a staircase.

Even happily mated persons have zipless-fuck fantasies once in a while. Women waiting for a traffic light may imagine a quick coupling with the cop on the corner. Men ordering coffee may picture themselves lifting the waitress's skirt and taking her from behind as she bends over the counter.

Most people keep these daydreams to themselves. Some couples, however, share this fantasy to bring the arousing idea of quick and anonymous sex with a stranger into their bedrooms. In their play, they rush frantically into hedonistic intercourse while pretending to meet for the first time. This game of make-believe gives them a brief vacation from their day-to-day relationship. In addition, it helps them retain the spice that brought them together in the first place.

ANNETTE AND HARVEY

Iris:

Annette is the owner of a boutique where I occasionally shop for clothing. Over the years we have gotten to know each other well enough to talk candidly about personal matters. I know, for example, that Annette and her boyfriend, Harvey, have no intention of getting married, although they have been living together for more than fifteen years. And she knows that Steve and I used to make our living writing adult fiction.

The last time I dropped into Annette's boutique, I mentioned that we were working on a collection of fantasies shared by happy couples in their intimate moments. Her face lit up.

"I've got a hot one for you," Annette said. "It's a fantasy game that Harvey and I have been playing for years . . ."

* * *

When Harvey was in college, he worked as a delivery boy for one of those very expensive Manhattan grocery stores. Most of their customers were rich women who were either too busy or too lazy to do their own shopping. They would phone in their orders, and Harvey or one of the other boys would deliver the groceries right to their apartment doors.

Some of them were so sex-starved that they would look for any excuse to invite Harvey in. They might offer him a cup of coffee or a cold drink, or ask him to carry the groceries into the kitchen. Anything to get him inside. I can understand it. Harvey was always handsome, with the kind of clean-cut good looks that drive that kind of woman wild.

Some of them would ask specifically for him when they called in their orders and then be brazen enough to come to the door dressed in sexy lingerie or even stark-naked. I'm sure that Harvey was easy to seduce. He always liked sex, and at that age any woman would have been hard to turn down.

All this happened before we met, but Harvey has told me all about it. As a matter of fact, I love to hear the details. I used to get all turned on when he described the way he would screw them on the living-room rug or against the dining-room wall. Sometimes they even made it to the bedroom.

One day after he and I had been living together for a few years, I got a crazy idea. I called Harvey at work and asked him to pick up a few things on the way home—you know, bread, milk, things like that. I double-locked the door so that he wouldn't be able to get in with his key. When he got home, I waited for him to knock.

"Just a minute, delivery boy," I called. "I'll be right with you." Then I opened the door wearing nothing but a towel wrapped around me as if I had just gotten out of the shower.

Harvey wore a big smile on his face. He's a fast learner and caught on immediately to what I had in mind. "Would you like me to bring this stuff into the kitchen for you, ma'am?" he asked.

"Yes, boy," I said in a sexy voice. "Please do." I let the towel slip a little bit, revealing the tops of my breasts.

Harvey looked me up and down as if he had never

seen my body before. "A beautiful woman like you must get kind of lonely," he said, following me into the kitchen.

"Yes," I answered. "My husband goes away on business trips very often, and I really don't get enough sex. Do you think you could help me out?" At this, I dropped the towel completely and stood there naked before him.

Harvey took me in his arms and kissed me passionately on the mouth. As our tongues dueled, I could feel him hard against me through his pants. "Hmmm," I murmured, reaching down to touch him. "You've got a big one. Hurry, I want it in me."

Moving backward, I pulled him until I felt the edge of the kitchen table against my bare ass. I leaned back so that the top half of my body was on the table. With my feet, I dragged over two chairs for me to rest my legs on.

Harvey stood wide-eyed, staring at the invitation offered by my open vagina. Quickly he unzipped his fly and took out his stiff penis. He never even took off his pants. Before I knew it, he was inside me, thrusting into me for all he was worth. I tried imagining myself as one of those bored rich women on his delivery route as he drove frantically in and out of me.

I could tell that he was really turned on, and for a moment I was afraid that he would come too fast. But before I knew it, my own climax began. I shouted and hollered as if it was the first sex I had gotten in months. And that did it for Harvey. In a second, he was hollering too. I wrapped my legs around his waist and pulled him tight against me.

"That was a wonderful surprise," he said later as he was zipping up his pants. "I'll be glad to make deliveries to this house anytime."

Now, whenever I feel like playing that fantasy game again, I just call him at work and ask for a delivery.

FAYE AND JOEL

Iris:

Faye and I have been friends for as long as I can remember. As adolescents, we kept no secrets from each other. In fact, just a few hours after Faye lost her virginity, she was on the phone telling me about it. What I love about Faye's dynamic personality is her enthusiasm and joy for life. She's always up for a new adventure.

Faye lives in Pennsylvania now, and we haven't gotten to see much of each other since I moved to California. A few years ago, when Steve was lecturing in Philadelphia, Faye and I met and had dinner together. During our conversation, she told me about a sex game that she and her husband, Joel, played, and asked what I thought about it. I must have shelved her story in some corner of my mind, because when Steve and I decided to write this book, Faye and Joel's fantasy was the first one I thought of. . . .

* * *

One of the guys Joel works with is recently divorced and is always on the make. He goes out every night looking for some kind of sexual encounter. He tells Joel about his experiences in lurid detail, and I always like it when Joel repeats the stories to me.

One night over dinner, Joel was telling me about his friend's latest conquest, and I found myself getting aroused. It seems his friend met some woman in a bar and ended up in bed with her after talking for only a few minutes. Somehow the idea really turned me on.

You know, Joel and I practically grew up together. By the time we had our first date, we had already known each other forever. The first time we made love, it seemed like the most natural thing in the world. You might say we had been building up to it for years. So the thought of making it with a total stranger within a few minutes of meeting was a novelty that got to me.

I was feeling kind of playful, so I got an idea for an adventurous little game. When I told Joel about it, he was all for it.

The next night we met at the bar of a downtown hotel, a place that had a reputation as a meat market, where singles go to pick each other up. He got there first. My heart was beating with excitement when I walked in. I had hardly ever gone into a bar alone before. And, besides, I knew I was going there to get picked up.

Joel was standing at the bar with a drink in front of him. I took a seat at the opposite end, making sure there was an empty stool next to me. I ordered a glass of white wine, expecting Joel to move in right away. But he didn't. He just sat there watching me in the mirror as I sipped my wine. There was a hungry look in his eyes, as if he was undressing me in his mind and devouring me on the spot.

His expression was exciting me, so I looked back at him in the mirror, meeting his eyes with mine. We smiled at each other for a while and flirted with each other's reflection. I was already on my second drink by the time Joel started toward me. Slipping into the seat beside me, he said, "Mind if I join you?"

I was trembling all over. "Please do," I said.

"I've been watching you all evening," he said.

His voice was husky and deep. I almost didn't recognize it. As I drained my glass, he waved at the bartender and ordered me another.

"You're a very beautiful woman," he said. "I find myself getting excited just looking at you."

When the bartender brought my third glass of wine, I felt Joel's hand brush lightly against my thigh. I liked the way his fingers moved in little circles. I could actually feel myself getting wet. I think part of it was the idea of being in a crowd like that. I know it never would have happened that fast at home.

Joel was really into his role as a stranger, and I was enjoying every minute of it. I had never been picked up in my life. And Joel had never flirted with me like that. I could feel my nipples hardening inside my bra. I wanted him, I think more than I ever wanted him before. My head was spinning from the wine, but that didn't stop me from asking him to order another.

"I've got a better idea," he said. "Why don't we have our drinks someplace where we can be alone?"

I genuinely felt nervous. "Like where?" I asked.

"Upstairs," he said. "I'll go get us a room."

Unable to speak, I just nodded.

I waited in the bar until Joe returned. He escorted me into the elevator and pressed number eleven. As the doors closed, he pulled me toward him and started kissing me passionately, pressing his body tightly against mine. While we kissed, he slid his hand up my dress and started feeling me all over. He had never done anything like that before outside of our own home. I heard the elevator doors opening and Joel's hand was still up inside my dress, but I was so excited that I didn't care if anybody saw us. I couldn't wait to get to the room. I wanted to rip his clothes off right there.

That's exactly what I did the second we were inside the hotel room. We were both frantic. We clawed at each other, getting rid of our clothing any way we could. We struggled and tore until we were half-undressed. I was so hot that I thought I would explode.

A moment later, we were rolling around on the floor like animals. First I was under him and then he was under me, all the time with him plunging in and out of me like a stallion. When I came, I screamed so loud I thought somebody was going to call the police. Later, when we caught our breath, he said, "What did you say your name was again?"

Well, what do you think? Is it weird or crazy? Because, to tell you the truth, we've done the same thing several times since then, and we intend to keep on doing it.

TRUDY AND OLIVER

Steve:

The New York City subway is an interesting place to observe human behavior. Because the conditions it creates are unlike any found in nature, most regular subway riders develop special strategies for dealing with them. During the rush hours, for example, people are packed together so tightly that it is possible to be in close physical contact with three or four strangers all at the same time. To avoid the embarrassment that might otherwise accompany this forced intimacy, seasoned commuters are careful to avoid looking directly into one another's faces: some read newspapers; others close their eyes and pretend to sleep; still others gaze out the window, even though nothing can be seen in the dark subway tunnels.

Once, when Iris and I were living in New York, I happened to be sharing these observations with Trudy, a neighbor. During our conversation, Trudy told me an interesting subway story. Although Trudy's story was about a pleasant experience she had with her husband Oliver, she began by describing an unpleasant one. . . .

* * *

Oliver and I both take the subway to and from work, but since we have different schedules, we don't usually travel together. One night on my way home, I was packed in with the other cattle as usual when I suddenly felt a hand on my backside. Well, you know, you get used to that sort of thing when you're jammed into a crowd twice a day. Most of the time it's an accident and the person attached to the hand is just as uncomfortable about it as you are. But this hand was moving slowly around in a way that made me think he might be doing it on purpose.

I say "he," although I'm not really sure that it was a man's hand. The crush had me pressed so tightly against two different men and one woman that I really couldn't tell which one it was. I put on an angry expression and glared at each of them, but the woman had her eyes closed, and both of the men were staring out the windows. For a few moments I tried to squirm away from the mystery hand, but each time I moved I realized that I was giving him or her another free feel. Finally, I just did my best to ignore it until the train came to my stop and I got out.

That night while we were eating dinner, I told Oliver what had happened. I was still angry, but Oliver thought the whole thing was kind of funny. "Look at it this way," he said. "I know you'd never *let* another man touch you that way, and I certainly wouldn't want you to. But on the subway, there's not much you can do about it. So, why not just enjoy it? When you think about it, you were getting a free feel yourself."

At first, his casual attitude made me mad. Here I was being abused, and he thought it was funny. As

I reflected, though, I realized that he was right in a perverted kind of way. After all, I wasn't really sure that the person on the train was doing it on purpose. And as long as I wasn't being deliberately violated, no real harm had been done. In a way it was kind of erotic to think of being felt up by a stranger in front of all those people.

I can't explain why, but our conversation excited me a little. As soon as the dinner dishes were done, I led Oliver into the bedroom for some really good sex. We didn't say anything more about the subway incident, but I think that Oliver understood that it had something to do with my arousal.

Anyway, about a week later, I was packed into the subway again when I felt a hand moving boldly over my backside. This one wasn't making any pretense at all. He was feeling me up as if he had a perfect right to do so. I was trying to decide whether to shout at him or stomp on his foot when I looked up and realized that it was Oliver. He was holding a newspaper in his free hand and pretending to read it while his other hand explored my bottom.

I was about to greet him when I realized that he was making believe he didn't know me. So I decided to play along. For a while I just held still while he gently rubbed my ass. Then I moved a little bit, showing him that it was as good for me as it was for him. Slowly, I turned until I was facing him. His hand sort of stayed in place so that it was now touching my crotch.

I took a quick look around to make sure that nobody was paying attention to what we were doing, and of course nobody was. As usual, everybody was pretending to be the only person in the world, reading the subway signs or gazing out the window and scrupulously avoiding direct visual contact with anybody else. After reassuring myself, I moved my own hand as unobtrusively as possible until it was right against the front of Oliver's pants. He was already hard, but I felt him getting harder under my touch.

We rode that way for quite a while, careful not to look at each other as we fondled each other's genitals. I was so excited that I thought I might actually have a climax. I could feel Oliver's penis pulsating and I was afraid that he would wet his pants if I kept it up. I don't think that would have stopped me, but by then the train was nearing our stop, and anyway the crowd was beginning to thin out.

When we got off the train, we continued acting like we didn't know each other until we had climbed the stairs into the street. Then Oliver turned to me with a look of mock surprise and said, "Trudy, I didn't expect to run into you. How's your day going?"

We both started laughing and we practically ran home to finish what we had started on the subway. We did, too, as soon as we got into the house. And as soon as it was over, we started again.

I don't really know why it was such a turn-on, but I do know that we've done the same thing again a few times since then. Some nights when we happen to be getting off work at the same hour, we arrange to meet at the subway station. We pretend not to know each other and get into the same subway car. Then we manage to get the crowd to press us together and we feel each other up until we get off the train and run home in a state of breathless excitement.

I bet you never thought the subway could be so much fun.

7   Tell Me About It

One of Shakespeare's best known tragedies is *Othello,* the tale of a Moorish nobleman in the service of Venice. As a result of an associate's villainous whisperings, Othello becomes convinced that his wife, Desdemona, is having an affair with one of the lieutenants in his force. Eventually, obsessed with jealousy, he kills Desdemona and himself. The idea is not a novel one. History is filled with stories of noble souls torn asunder by irrational jealousy.

In 1541, for example, England's King Henry VIII ordered the execution of two men after his wife Catherine admitted that she had slept with them. The jealous king demanded the removal of their heads even though the transgression occurred while Catherine was a teenager and before she had met Henry. The following year, his majesty contrived to execute his wife as well.

The French philosopher René Descartes said that jealousy is one of six unlearned human emotions. Modern psychologists disagree. They believe that jealousy is a hybrid of learned emotions, all rooted in the anxiety that results from feeling unloved or unwanted. Many human beings learn jealousy by the time they are two years old.

In a child, this learning process often begins with the arrival of a new brother or sister. When the parents give attention to the baby, the older child may feel that they have stopped loving him or her. The result is anger, frustration, and insecurity.

The situation is only slightly different when an adult thinks about his or her mate giving sexual attention to another partner. Like the child with a new sibling, the jealous lover loses confidence and self-respect, doubting that he or she measures up to the mate's other partners. As King Henry demonstrated, this may happen even though the event occurred before their marriage. The resulting insecurity can haunt a relationship, destroying it as finally—if not as dramatically—as it destroyed the marriage of Othello and Desdemona.

Few marriages are immune from the problems of jealousy. Modern sex researchers have found that many Americans engage in premarital sex with partners other than those whom they eventually marry. When husbands and wives learn this about each other, they have to deal with the potential jealousy that may result.

Some of the couples to whom we spoke found that they could avoid feelings of anger, frustration, and insecurity by turning negative responses into positive ones. They frankly discuss relationships that preexisted their marriages, even deriving sexual pleasure by talking about them. A few report that fantasizing about their spouses' premarital experiences makes them feel more secure, because, after all, their mates ended up by choosing them.

JUDY AND MARK

Iris:

I met Judy while attending exercise classes at a women's fitness center. We took to each other almost immediately and purposely scheduled our classes together so that we could meet. After vigorous workouts, we would relax in the soothing Jacuzzi and make idle comments to each other about the women there. We became good friends and spoke freely about all the half-naked bodies around us and their different shapes and sizes.

One rainy day, when very few women showed up, we found that we were the only two sitting in the Jacuzzi. Judy began talking about one of our exercise instructors and what a beautiful body she had. Suddenly she asked, "Have you ever had sex with another woman?" Before I could answer, she said, "I did once, when I was a teenager. I haven't done anything like that since then, but I still get a thrill telling my husband Mark about it, and it really turns him on to hear it . . ."

* * *

I was going on sixteen and I had a job as a junior counselor at a summer camp. One day we took the campers on an overnight tent outing and I shared a tent with Arlene, one of the other junior counselors.

Arlene was about the same age as I was, but she was very well developed. She was really stacked, with a pair of enormous tits that caught the attention of all the guys and were the envy of every girl in camp.

It was nighttime and we had a small light on in the tent. We were tired from a hard day of setting up for all the kids. When Arlene started to undress, I found myself looking at her beautiful naked breasts. I was in awe of them.

Arlene laughed when she saw me staring. "What do you think of my tits?" she asked.

"God," I blurted, "They're just magnificent. I wish mine were like that."

Lowering her voice, she said slyly, "Why don't you touch them?"

I was too embarrassed to do anything but stand there like a frozen statue, still staring.

"Go ahead," she coaxed, moving closer. "Touch them." She walked toward me and took my hand in hers.

Before I knew it, I was holding them. I could feel her nipples hardening against my palms. As I fondled them, I could see by the expression on Arlene's face that she was thoroughly enjoying it. "Why don't you take off your top too," she said. "And I'll show you how good it feels." Without even thinking about it, my fingers unbuttoned my blouse and unhooked my bra.

"You've got nice tits, too," Arlene said.

"Nothing like yours," I replied in a whisper as my hands returned to her mounds.

"Yes," she said proudly. "Mine are rather large, aren't they? But yours are nice and firm." As she spoke, she reached out and took my breasts in her hands. She seemed to know exactly what she was doing, and I tried to imitate her movements. She held my nipples between her thumbs and forefingers and rolled them gently, first one and then the other. I had played with myself, of course, but it never felt so good as this.

"Have you ever done this before?" I asked.

"Oh, yes," she said. "Lots of times. I'm no virgin. Are you?"

I didn't answer, but it must have been obvious that I was.

After we handled each other's tits for a few minutes, she suggested that we take off the rest of our clothes, unroll our sleeping bags, and lie down so that we could be comfortable. A moment later we were both nude and lying side by side. I reached for her breasts again, but she took one of my hands and guided it down to her pubic mound. Trembling, I pressed my palm flat against it. Her hair wasn't as tightly curled as mine was there, but it felt soft as I ran my fingers through it.

"Put your finger deep inside me," she instructed. When I felt the warm wetness of her, I put my finger in as far as it would reach. "Now, touch my clit," she commanded.

I had heard about the clit, but I really didn't know exactly what it was. As I fumbled around, Arlene sensed my ignorance.

"Haven't you ever masturbated?" she asked.

"Sure I have," I answered.

"Did you have an orgasm?" she asked.

I stuttered and admitted that I really wasn't certain.

"Well, tonight you're going to have one for sure," she said. "I promise. Now you just lie there and let me do it to you."

I let go of Arlene's luscious body with some disappointment, but her promise filled me with anticipation. I lay back as she commanded, and she began to stroke me lightly. First she just touched my tits, making little circles around my nipples with her fingertips. Then she started drawing her hand softly over my belly and down toward my vagina.

She rubbed my mound and gently petted the lips. I could feel myself opening up to her touch. When she slipped a finger inside me, I thought I would die from pleasure. But it just kept getting better.

She traced the puffy opening of my slit with her moistened finger, moving it upward. As she got closer to the top, the pleasure increased, intensifying my chills. I had never felt anything like this before. Never.

"There," she whispered as she stroked my little button. "There's your clit."

The more she played with it, the harder it got. I almost cried with excitement. "You can make yourself feel this good any time you want," Arlene said. "All you have to do is touch yourself in just the right place."

As she spoke, she teased my clit with her fingers. First she touched it lightly. Then she made figure eights around it. Then she dipped into my open slit for more moisture and rubbed it gently into my button. Each time I thought I couldn't stand it anymore, she changed her approach and made it feel even better.

A strange new sensation was building in me. It was unlike anything I had ever experienced before. It was like something growing, pushing against my insides in all directions at once. I felt like crying and laughing and giggling and fainting all at the same time. I was scared. "No," I mumbled. "No."

Then it hit me. I felt something inside me shatter, and all the tension I had ever known was suddenly draining out of me, flowing through my body. I sobbed and moaned, wishing that Arlene's finger would stop churning and hoping that it would go on forever. When it ended, I was in a dream state.

"That was an orgasm," Arlene whispered. But I knew it even before she said so. "After you give me one, I'll give you another."

I couldn't believe that I'd ever be able to go through an experience like that again. But Arlene assured me that I'd be ready in no time. Meanwhile, she showed me how to do it to her. At first, I was ashamed to handle her pussy the way she handled mine. After a few moments, though, the shame was replaced by excitement. When I brought her to climax with my finger, I had a sense of triumph. I had come of age.

We spent the whole night taking turns getting each other off. Neither of us slept a wink before the sun came up. But I was filled with energy.

That's the only time in my life that I had a sex experience with another woman. But I still get excited whenever I think about it. I've told Mark about it lots of times, and he always gets really aroused too. He likes me to tell him about the tiniest details, and I love to do it.

Sometimes he points to a picture in a sexy magazine or at some cutie on the beach or something and asks whether Arlene looked anything like her. Then I know that he wants me to talk about it. Once in a while he gets so hot while I'm telling him that he handles himself until he's right at the brink of orgasm. Then I have to stop talking for a while to give him a chance to calm down. But as soon as he does, I go on with the story.

Sometimes, when I happen to be at my horniest, Mark says he's too tired for sex. When that happens, I know that all I have to do is start talking about Arlene and he'll soon forget how tired he is and give me all the hot sex I can handle.

RICHARD AND ELLEN

Steve:

Richard, an accountant, has been preparing tax returns for Iris and me for the past fifteen years. Every tax season when I meet with him to go over our return, he jokes about how nice it must be to make a living thinking about sex and asks what projects we are working on at the moment. This year, when I told him we were preparing a collection of couples' sex fantasies, he chuckled.

"I've got a hot one for you," he said. "Knowing my wife, Ellen, you're never going to believe it."

I didn't really know Ellen, having been introduced to her only a few times. I said so and added that I've learned never to be surprised about the sexual fantasies or sexual activities of anybody, no matter who they are or how they seem on the surface. Richard chuckled again and started to talk . . .

* * *

When Ellen and I first met, she was rather inexperienced. She came from a strict religious upbringing and believed that nice girls don't screw until after they're married. She had dated a few men, but never got serious enough with any of them to sacrifice her precious virginity.

On the other hand, I was brought up to believe that on judgment day the thing a man regrets most is his missed opportunities. So I started screwing around when I was a kid and kept it up until I met Ellen. Since then, I swear I haven't had any woman but her. And we've been married now for, what, twenty-two years.

Anyway, when we first started going together, she knew about my past. The idea that I'd screwed lots of women fascinated her. She used to ask me about it all the time, but I refused to talk about it because I thought it would be ungentlemanly. Finally, about a year after we were married, I broke down one night when she started asking, and told her about some of the lady friends I'd had.

Well, it didn't take long for me to realize that I had stepped into quicksand. At first the stories were making her hot, and she started asking for more details. But then she began to get jealous, and before I knew it, she was trying to pick a fight with me. I stopped talking about it right away, of course, but that night was a disaster.

Then, about a week later, she started asking again. This time I was kind of torn. There was no way I wanted to take a chance of getting her angry again. But at the same time I remembered how excited she had gotten in the beginning, and I wanted to find a way to recapture that mood. So I took a chance and told her about my first time. I was only fifteen, and it was with a paid hooker.

I could see by her response that this was the right idea. It was a way for me to talk about another woman without making her feel threatened or jealous. The fact that it was a paid hooker reassured her that there was no emotional involvement; it was purely physical. Ellen got so excited that she gave me a night like I never had before. Ever since then, whenever we want something really special, I tell her again about me and that hooker.

I was only fifteen at the time. An older friend of mine had raved about this prostitute, saying that she'd be the perfect one to break my virginity. He even made the appointment for me.

When I got to her place, she answered the door in a robe. As soon as I stepped inside, she took it off and was naked. She was in her mid-twenties and a little on the chubby side, with huge round tits.

She put my hands on her tits and undressed me while I played with them. I was so hard that she must have had trouble getting my pants off. After she did, she got down on her knees on the floor and started licking my cock. I stared in amazement. I had heard of blowjobs, but I couldn't believe I was actually getting one. After she sucked me for a minute or two, I thought I was going to come in her mouth. But she stopped just in time and walked over to the bed.

I didn't know what to do next, so I just stood there and looked as she lay back and spread her legs. I went to the bed and she reached up to pull me down on top of her. She took my dick in her hand and guided it into her.

When I felt myself sliding into her, I couldn't believe it was really happening. The thrill of finally being inside a woman's pussy was more than I could stand. I was so excited that I came right away. It was over before it even started.

Ellen likes this story. She says that even when I'm not talking about it, she sometimes thinks about it while we're having sex. She likes to picture me as a kid with this experienced hooker. She says that hearing about it and thinking about it makes it easier for her to have an orgasm.

God only knows what this hooker really looked like. I don't even remember. I've described it all to Ellen so many times and changed it so much over the years that there isn't much reality left in it anymore. It's become pure fantasy. But it works like a voodoo love charm for both of us.

CATHY AND JASON

Iris:

One of the toughest things about being a writer is not having a steady income. When Steve and I were writing adult fiction, there were times when we would go for months without selling a manuscript. Then one of us would have to look for a job. When it was my turn, I usually found work in sales.

When I was employed as a sales representative for a temporary service agency, my fellow workers learned of my career as an X-rated novelist. I took quite a bit of ribbing about it from everyone except Cathy, the young office manager. Cathy seemed to think that a writer of sex books was like some kind of sex therapist. This probably explains why she was willing to tell me intimate details about her marital life. One morning, after her husband, Jason, had dropped her at the office, I commented on his good looks.

Cathy sighed. "Yes, everybody thinks so," she said. "When we first started going out together, I just couldn't imagine what such a handsome guy could see in me . . ."

* * *

When we were in college, Jason was on the football team and could have any girl he wanted. In fact, he usually did. He used to go out with three or four different girls a week. All of them beautiful.

I wasn't all that popular. You might say I was kind of a bookworm. When Jason needed help in one of his subjects, the college tutoring service recommended me, and that's how we got to know each other. After three tutoring sessions, he asked me out. I couldn't believe it. A few weeks later, we started going steady. From that time on, Jason never dated another woman.

It's funny, he never even tried to kiss me until we had gotten serious with each other. One night after we were married, I asked him why. He said that all the other girls he had gone out with were easy lays, and he respected me because I was so different. Well, I got kind of curious and asked him to tell me about some of the others. When he refused, I pulled down our college yearbook and insisted that he show me all the girls he had been with.

Hesitantly, he turned the pages, pointing out some of his old girlfriends. But that didn't satisfy me. I wanted him to give me all the gory details. At first, it was like pulling teeth, but eventually he became more comfortable with the idea. As he spoke about the things he had done with this one or that one, I got real excited and began stroking him through his pants.

He said, "Hey, I thought this was something men weren't supposed to tell their wives about."

"Maybe they're not," I answered. "But I like it. Tell me more. I want to hear about it. It turns me on."

He found a picture of the cheerleading squad and pointed to a cute blonde. I remember her. "She was something else," he said. "She had these great big boobs that bounced up and down when she did her cheers. She liked to take me under the bleachers at the football field and pull up her sweater so I could suck her huge pink nipples. Then she'd put my cock between her tits and rub me up and down until I came all over her."

I could just picture it happening in my mind. Instead of making me jealous, it got me even more aroused. I wanted him to do the same things to me that he had done to her. Quickly, I took off my top and bra and started rubbing my own nipples while he watched. "Come on," I said. "You did it to her; now do it to me."

I didn't even give him a chance to get his pants off. I just opened his fly and pulled out his cock. Getting onto my knees in front of the couch, I licked his cock until it was covered with saliva. Then I pressed my breasts around it. I moved my body up and down slowly, fucking him with my tits. Each time the heat of his cock came near my mouth, I reached out with my tongue and gave it a lick. All the time, I was looking at the picture of the blonde in the yearbook, imagining him with her.

He must have seen me looking, because he groaned and said, "Oh, you do it so much better than she did."

His words made me feel like the sexiest woman in the world. I wasn't the least bit jealous of the cheerleader, because I had him and she didn't. And I was much better at loving Jason than she could ever be. He had just told me so himself.

"What else did you do with her?" I asked softly. I wanted more stimulus for my imagination.

This time Jason didn't hesitate. "Sometimes she'd bend over and I'd fuck her from behind," he said. I could feel his cock throb with excitement as he remembered. "She really used to throw that ass back at me when we did it."

I stood up and pulled down my pants and panties, leaving them bunched up around my ankles. Then, standing in front of the couch, I bent way over. I knew that he could see my open crack. "Come on," I said. "Show me how you did it to Miss Cheerleader."

He jumped to his feet and moved forward against me. I could feel his hard-on jabbing at the crease between my buttocks. Then he took it in his hand and guided it lower until he found my pussy. With one quick thrust, he drove into me. At the same moment, I threw my ass back at him.

I was trying to do it the way I imagined she did. Only I wanted to be better. Reaching back between my legs, I cupped his balls in my hand and massaged them lightly.

"Did she do this?" I asked.

"No," he said. "Nobody's ever done me as good as you. You're the best."

At that, we both started to climax. He pumped and pumped until I thought it would never stop. I could feel our mingled juices filling me and overflowing to run down my legs. When it was over, we both fell back onto the couch and laughed.

That yearbook has become our favorite book ever since. It's a fantastic stimulant for our sex lives. Whenever we feel like a really hot time, one of us gets out the yearbook and starts turning pages.

8

Look at What They're Doing

There's an old joke about parents who ask their son what he wants for his birthday. When the child says, "I wanna watch," his parents decide to let him. Some call it a meaningless play on words. Others see a profound statement about the human condition in the parents' misunderstanding of their child's meaning—if, indeed, it was a misunderstanding.

To some extent, most of us are curious about what other people look like in the nude or when they are making love. Some seek pleasure by satisfying their curiosity. Behaviorists say that this is normal, and call such people scopophiles, a term derived from the Greek word *skoptos,* which means "to view," and the Latin root *philia,* which means "love of."

Many lay persons use a different name, however, expressing a contempt that goes all the way back to the English legend of Lady Godiva. According to this tale, Lord Leofric, an eleventh-century earl, was taxing his subjects so heavily that many were reduced to starvation. When his wife, Godiva, begged him to relent, Leofric sneered and said sarcastically the he would lower taxes on the day she rode naked on horseback through the town of Coventry.

The lady, moved by her love for the people, announced that she would comply with her husband's condition. On the day of her ride, she asked the residents of Coventry to remain indoors with their curtains drawn and their eyes closed. All the townsfolk honored her request except Tom the tailor, who could not resist the urge to sneak a peek. Tom lost his eyesight as a result, and ever since, people who like to watch have been called Peeping Toms.

Historians claim that there is no truth in the legend of Lady Godiva. Leofric, they say, was a benevolent sort of a fellow who would never have overtaxed his subjects or humiliated his wife. Tom, the peeping tailor, was a villain who never even existed. Fictional or otherwise, however, it is significant that Tom is remembered as a scoundrel and that his name is given to those who enjoy seeing others engage in sexual intimacy.

None of this makes the desire to watch go away. At best, it drives that desire underground. We may not actually stand on milk crates to peer into bedroom windows, but almost everyone imagines it once in a while.

Some of the couples we talked to admitted that they indulge in scopophilic fantasies. They lie together imagining that they are watching couples or groups of people engaging in sex acts. They whisper descriptions to each other until their shared fantasy leads them into sex acts of their own. In this way, they enjoy their scopophilia without ever really becoming Peeping Toms.

JENNIFER AND ADAM

Iris:

When Steve and I first arrived in the Golden State, California was in the middle of a real-estate boom. We heard many stories about people whose homes had doubled or even tripled in value in just a few years. Since our income from writing was not always steady, I decided to cash in on the bull market by becoming a real-estate agent. As luck would have it, however, the boom ended before I got my license. Consequently, I ended up sitting in a real-estate office with a lot of time on my hands.

Jennifer worked in the same office and was a veteran who had weathered many cycles in the real-estate market. She assured me that, if I was patient, things would improve before long. While we waited, we passed hours together in conversation. When I told her about the adult novels Steve and I had written, she expressed more interest than most people do. Suddenly she smiled. "I was just thinking about my old college roommate Sandy," she said. "Now, that girl was a walking pornographic novel. Whenever my husband, Adam, and I need something to spice up our love life, we talk about Sandy."

"Why don't you tell me about it," I coaxed. But from the expression on Jennifer's face, I could see that she didn't need any coaxing. . . .

* * *

I didn't know Sandy until we were assigned to the same apartment in a dormitory at State College. We got along so well that we roomed together for the next four years. Actually, we were really quite different. I was a studious type, but for Sandy college was strictly a social event. While I was working on my grades, she was working on a list of all the guys she had dated. It seemed like she had a different boyfriend every week.

Sometimes, while I was in my own room studying, I would hear sounds coming from Sandy's room that let me know she had brought a date home. This almost always meant that she would end up having sex with him. Usually I would hear giggling and soft voices for a while, followed by the sounds of heavy breathing and finally by grunts and moans. Since I didn't do much dating at the time, I found it all very distracting.

At first, I was kind of resentful. I told myself that it was because she was disturbing my peace and quiet. I guess the real reason was that I was envious. After a while, though, my resentment turned into an excited curiosity. I would sit at my desk with a book in front of me, but all my attention was centered on the sounds coming from Sandy's room. I found myself daydreaming, trying to imagine exactly what they were doing. Sometimes, guilt would drive me back to my studies, but it was hard to concentrate.

Well, one night the sounds of heavy breathing seemed to fill the apartment, and the moaning was so loud that I couldn't overcome my curiosity. I tiptoed over to Sandy's door so that I could hear better and found that the door was open about two inches. I tried to tear myself away, but it was hopeless. I really had no choice; I just had to look in. Holding my breath, I pressed my eye to the opening.

When I did, I almost gave myself away by gasping

in shock. Sandy and her date were both totally naked. He was lying on his back with his feet toward the door. Sandy was sitting on his chest with her back to me. Since her body was blocking his face, I felt safe, knowing that neither of them could see me watching.

For a while, I just stared at his loins. He had a tremendous erection, and it was sticking straight up into the air. I didn't have a lot of sexual experience, so I was fascinated by the sight of male sex organs. His was huge, and it was throbbing and pulsating like a living thing. I got so excited watching it that I forgot to hold my breath.

At first, I couldn't imagine why Sandy wasn't paying any attention to his penis. Then, slowly, I realized what they were doing. He was eating her. She kept rocking forward, grinding her naked backside against him. Each time she let out a husky moan, I imagined what his tongue must be doing inside her.

When they started to change position, I ran back to my room, afraid of being caught. But there was no hope of getting any studying done. My mind was spinning with erotic images. For the next week, all I could think about was what I had seen. I sat in classes like a zombie, with an attentive expression on my face but only one thing on my mind.

The following Friday, Sandy had a new boyfriend in her room. This time, I remained quietly at my desk, deliberately listening for sounds of passion. For a time I heard nothing at all and thought I was going to be disappointed. Then their rhythmic breathing began coming through the wall. I waited until I was sure they would be too involved to hear me, and stole quietly to their door. To my dismay, I found it closed.

I was so frustrated that, for a moment, I thought of trying to peek in the keyhole, but of course there was no keyhole. I was about to return to my room when, in desperation, I pressed my hand softly against the door. It wasn't latched. Carefully, I pushed it open just enough so that I could see inside. The door squeaked slightly, but Sandy and her boyfriend were too preoccupied to notice.

Sandy was lying on her back with her legs spread. He was between them, humping furiously. Her calves were up and braced against his shoulders, opening her vulva wide. What a sight to behold. I could see his scrotum swinging forward and back as he drove in and out of her. I could see the muscles in his buttocks tensing and relaxing with each thrust. Sandy's explosive cries were keeping time with his movements. Every time he plunged into her, she groaned. I was filled with excitement as I imagined what Sandy must be feeling. I stood there for a long time, tingling all over. I was terrified that they might suddenly turn and see me, but it was impossible for me to leave. I stayed long enough to hear the sounds of Sandy's climax before my fear got the better of me and I crept back to my room.

For the next few days, my mind whirled in chaos. I couldn't concentrate on anything. All I could think about was what I had seen and what I would see next. I had already made up my mind to peek at Sandy and her date whenever I could. I couldn't wait for it to happen again. Three nights later, it did.

This time I actually had to turn the knob to get the

door open. My hands were trembling and my throat was dry, but nothing could stop me. My lustful curiosity knew no bounds. The sight that greeted me almost made me faint with arousal. I could actually see his penis sliding in and out of her. I stared hypnotized as her pelvis rocked.

Her opening was surrounded by bushy hair, plastered wetly against her skin. Her vagina clasped at his shaft, embracing it tightly as she rode him up and down. Once or twice, she moved so violently that he slipped out of her. I could see the swollen head of his organ coated with moisture. It was especially arousing for me to see her reach down and take it in her hand so that she could slip it back inside of her.

Both of them started moaning in accelerating rhythm, and I knew they were going to come. I stood riveted to the spot, my eyes fastened to the sight. A moment later, he shouted, "Oh, yes," and she cried, "Me too." They rolled and bucked, until I could see what looked like a river of semen running out of her around his pumping organ. Watching, I almost came with them. I was in such a daze that afterward, when I found myself back in my room, I really didn't know how I got there.

I lay in bed for hours, thinking about the scenes I had witnessed and burning with sexual excitement. Eventually, though, I began to feel guilty. I had committed a terrible invasion of Sandy's privacy. I felt a great need to confess, to tell Sandy what I had done and to ask her to make less noise in the future so that I wouldn't be tempted to do it again.

I waited until morning when we were having coffee together alone at our little dinette table. I stammered and beat around the bush for a while, and then finally I just blurted out the whole truth. Sandy didn't say a word until I was finished. Then she smiled and said the weirdest thing.

"That really turns me on," she whispered in a husky voice. "To know that you were watching while I fucked and sucked those guys. I love it. I just love it. I wish I had known while I was doing it. I think it would have made me even hotter. Next time, maybe I'll just leave the door open."

I didn't really know if she meant it or not. But a few days later, she proved that she did. She was getting ready to go out on a date when she said, "Jennifer, I've got a great idea for tonight. I'm going to tell my date that you're out and that we have the whole apartment to ourselves. Then, when I bring him back here, I'll leave the bedroom door wide open. You wait until we're really into it and then you can watch to your heart's content. Just be careful not to let him see you."

I never saw Sandy as hot as she was that night with her date. It was like she was performing especially for me. From the shadows in the hallway outside her room, I watched as she licked his entire naked body. He lay on his back trembling and quivering as she drew her tongue slowly over his neck and chest, stopping to suck sensuously at his nipples. She worked her mouth all the way down to his toes, dabbing her tongue lightly at his genitals as she went. On the way back up, she took his penis in her lips and moved it slowly up and down inside her mouth. She was facing me, and I could swear that she gave me a little wink as she sucked him.

After tonguing him for what seemed like an eternity, Sandy whispered something that I couldn't hear and got onto her knees on the bed. Her bottom was toward me and I could see the bright red gash of her vagina spread open and covered with moisture. He got onto his knees behind her. His penis was stiff and hard and stood straight out in front of him, pointing directly at her opening. Slowly, he moved forward, using his hand to position its tip against her labia. Then, with a thrust of his buttocks, he drove himself inside.

Sandy sighed as he began pumping into her, doggie-style.

I had heard of this position before, but I had never really imagined what it looked like. I couldn't believe that I was actually seeing it live before me. Their rhythmic cries filled the air in time with the movements of their combined loins. It was really getting to me. I wished I was Sandy, feeling a man's stiff penis pumping inside me.

Just when I thought I had seen everything, he pulled out of her vagina and began coating his penis with baby oil from a bottle Sandy handed him. He applied it with long strokes, closing his eyes and shuddering a little at the pleasure of his own touch. When the shaft and head were glistening, he began using his fingers to apply the oil to the crack of Sandy's anus. This could only mean one thing, and the thought of it made me shake.

Inching forward on his knees, he began rubbing the end of his organ up and down in the oiled furrow between her buttocks. Sandy's moans were becoming louder as he forced her open ever so slowly. He remained with his penis poised at the tightly puckered little hole, hunching himself slightly forward and back. Then, before my eyes, the bulbous head of his organ disappeared into her anus. Sandy grunted with a mixture of pleasure and pain.

Only the tip was inside, and I could still see his white shaft, stiff and hard, like a pole separating their bodies.

"More," Sandy screamed. "Give me more. Shove more of it inside me."

Almost teasingly, he pushed forward against her, burying another fraction of an inch, but still leaving most of his shaft outside. Her bottom was bobbing up and down, gulping for more of his stiff penis. His scrotum swung forward to bump against her backturned vulva as he slowly slid more of himself inside. It seemed to take forever, but eventually, he was buried to the hilt in her tight anus. I couldn't imagine how she could stand it.

The screams and moans coming from that room were not to be believed. Sandy threw herself back at him as if she wanted still more. I had never seen her that excited, and I wondered whether it was because she knew I was watching or because it really felt so pleasurable to have him inside that part of her. I wondered whether she had done it this way before or whether it was something she concocted just to give me a show.

Gradually, the tempo of his thrusts increased until they seemed to be moving against each other at a frantic pace. My initial shock had worn off, and now it seemed almost natural for his penis to be in her anus. As he humped into her, he reached around her with one arm. I couldn't see his hand at work, but from the sounds Sandy was making, I knew that he had started to play with her clitoris. "I'm going to come," she shouted. "Keep fucking my ass. I'm going to come."

He began to groan in a hoarse lustful voice, and I could see his toes curl. I knew that he was having a climax. The thought of his sperm shooting deep into her bowel was inflaming my body. I stood mesmerized as my roommate thrashed back against the spurting penis that penetrated her anus. Without realizing it, I was pressing my hand against my vagina through my clothes. I waited until his flaccid organ slipped from between her buttocks, trailing a sticky string of semen.

When I was sure they were finished, I rushed back to my room, where I lay on my bed masturbating to relieve the tension that had built inside me. As my fingers whipped my own juices to a froth, I thought about what I had seen. All of the erotic sights blended into a blur of excitement, but I think that the most arousing part of all was that she knew I had been watching.

During the next three years, my own social life improved and I dated several different guys. But I still spent lots of time outside Sandy's bedroom door, watching and learning. The things I saw would fill a book.

A few years after college, I met Adam. We went out for about three months and then got married. I kept up my friendship with Sandy, and we get together with her frequently. One night, after having dinner with Sandy, Adam and I were home in bed when Adam made some comment about what a good body Sandy has.

"Does she look as good out of her clothes as she does in them?" he asked. "You must have seen her naked when you roomed together."

"Did I ever," I answered. "I've seen Sandy's body in positions you couldn't even begin to imagine."

I could see from the gleam in Adam's eye that my remark had aroused his curiosity. At first, when he asked me for details, I was evasive. I was a little bit embarrassed about admitting that I had been such a Peeping Tom. But he insisted in a way that made it clear that what he suspected was turning him on. So I started telling him about the days when Sandy and I were roommates.

I started out real vague, saying only that I had occasionally seen her in bed with men. But he kept probing and I kept telling him a little more. It seemed that the more truth I gave him, the more excited he became. Before long, I lost my embarrassment completely and told him detail by detail about all the things I had seen in Sandy's room.

That first time, I talked mostly about seeing her having anal intercourse. I could feel steamy passion coming from Adam's body as I spoke. I knew that he was fantasizing about Sandy naked and in heat, but that didn't bother me at all. He was more excited than I ever remember, and I loved the idea that I was arousing him with my words. The more I talked, the hotter he got. That night, our sex was better than it had been in a long time. I continued describing Sandy's exploits as we made love. We experienced erotic pleasures never known to us before.

Talking about what I saw Sandy and her dates doing was like a golden wand waving over our sex life. It was fantastic. We both realized immediately that we had found a sex game we were going to play forever. And we've been playing it ever since. Sandy doesn't know it, of course, but Adam and I watch her having sex whenever we want to. All we have to do is talk about it and let our imaginations take over. It gets better each time we do it.

NEIL AND SHEILA

Steve:

Neil is an investment counselor who has occasionally given advice to Iris and me. Once, when we were discussing retirement plans, I asked him what sort of arrangements he was making for his own retirement. I was surprised when he said that he and his wife, Sheila, hoped to own and operate a small motel.

"I thought you'd be sitting back and collecting dividends on all your investments," I said. "There can't be much money in a small motel. And if you're going to operate it yourselves, I don't imagine that it would pay enough to be worth your while?"

"You're right," Neil exclaimed. "The truth is that we could live on our investment income alone. The motel idea is just a fantasy. But we have a lot of fun with it.''

At the word "fantasy," I perked up my ears and mentioned our book.

"I'll tell you about our fantasy," Neil said with a laugh. "But if you're going to use it in your book, maybe I ought to negotiate for a piece of the action . . .''

* * *

It all started a few years ago when we were on vacation. We were driving the Pacific Coast Highway from California to Oregon, stopping at the poshest hotels we could find along the way. One night, while we were staying at a very nice place overlooking the ocean, we happened to glance up and were amazed by the stars. You never see as many in the city as you do when you're in the country. Anyway, the sky looked so beautiful that we decided to watch it from the outdoor whirlpool spa. It was pretty late, so we figured we'd have the pool to ourselves and we'd just be able to lounge in the water and gaze at the Milky Way.

We put on our bathing suits and strolled out toward the spa. As we approached, we saw that there was a couple already in it. Sheila wanted to return to our room, and we were just about to do so when I noticed that the woman in the spa was barebreasted.

"Wait a minute," I said. "Look at this.''

Trying not to be seen, we stood quietly watching them. A moment later, we both realized that the woman was completely nude and so was the man with her. They were unaware that they had an audience and were fooling around uninhibitedly like a couple of kids. They would splash and play in the water for a few seconds and then he would lean over and suck her nipple or something. At one point, he stood and picked her up in his arms, lifting the bottom half of her out of the water. She wrapped her legs around his, and I'm almost positive that I saw him enter her.

I've always been a secret peeper, so I was enjoying the show. But Sheila was starting to feel a little uncomfortable. She kept saying, "Come on, Neil, let's go back to the room." I knew that if I didn't take action immediately, I would miss the rest.

Sprinting forward, I shouted, "Come on in, Sheila," and I jumped into the whirlpool. I never saw two such shocked people in all my life. The woman unwrapped her legs and slid down until the water was up to her chin. But in spite of the Jacuzzi's ferocious bubbling, I could still see her tits bobbing up and down under the surface. And I could see his cock, standing out in erect frustration.

I just smiled innocently at them, trying to wear a Jack Nicholson smirk that would say, "I caught you." I could see from their expressions that they knew that I knew. And they knew that I knew that they knew that I knew. Then I called Sheila again.

Reluctantly, but not knowing what else to do, Sheila came and joined me in the pool. For a moment, the air was filled with embarrassed silence. Then the man said, "Hi. Enjoy the spa. We were just leaving."

I've really got to admire the guts of the guy. He stepped out of the Jacuzzi with dignity, as if he wasn't stark-naked and as if his stiff dick wasn't swinging from one side to the other. He carefully wrapped himself in a towel, taking his time and not showing any signs of discomfort. Then he held another towel spread open for the woman. She also put on an air of quiet dignity, stepping into the towel and allowing him to wrap her in it without turning to face us.

To tell you the truth, I looked without shame and I really got an eyeful. As she ascended the steps of the Jacuzzi, I could see her ass and her wet pussy quite clearly. Sheila glanced away, her face flushed with embarrassment. But I knew that she had taken a good look at the man's cock as he was getting out, too.

When they walked off, Sheila whispered, "How could you be so mean? They must be horribly embarrassed."

I laughed. "I couldn't help it," I said. "I just had to get a closer look. And, anyway, we don't appear to have upset them all that much." I pointed to the couple, now walking slowly into the hotel, arm in arm and dressed only in their towels. They were jokingly grabbing at each other and seemed to be having a lot of fun. "Look." I said to Sheila. "He's got his hand on her ass right now. They're going back to their room to finish what they started out here."

Sheila moved up against me in the water. "Do you think so?" she asked. I could tell that the whole incident was turning her on. "Wouldn't it be nice if we could watch them?" she said breathlessly. "But privately. Without their knowing it. Like on closed-circuit TV or something."

I sensed her excitement. Taking her in my arms, I whispered, "Let's go back to our own room and talk about it some more, before we get carried away and somebody catches us out here the way we caught them."

We practically ran back to our room, giggling all the way. As soon as we got inside, we tore off our bathing suits and threw ourselves down on the bed. As we stroked each other, we whispered about what we had seen in the pool. Then, pointing to the TV screen, I said, "Watch the TV and see what they're doing now." I started describing the woman as I had seen her in the pool, with her breasts exposed and her dark nipples erect. As I spoke, Sheila got more and more aroused.

I continued the description, talking about the man's cock and how hard it had been. I could hear Sheila's breathing become hoarse and labored. I began to improvise. I talked about the couple in bed in their hotel room, the woman's hand stroking the man's swollen hard-on. I described the way her pussy looked as he slid his fingers inside it. All the while I kept looking toward the TV screen and acting as though I could actually see what I was describing.

"Wouldn't it really be something to see this on our TV," Sheila said breathlessly. "There must be lots of people making love in their rooms at this very moment. Wouldn't it be exciting if we could watch them all? Especially the ones who came to the hotel specifically for sex."

As she spoke, I continued stroking her. She was getting wetter and wetter. Then, suddenly, to her surprise as well as mine, she let out a cry and began to climax. It had never happened so fast or so un-expectedly before. For me, it was a real thrill, be-cause I had hardly done anything to her. Just a few words and a little idle touching had been all it took to get her off. I kept rubbing her gently until she finished coming, and then I kept it up. Within mo-ments, she was climbing toward another orgasm.

By now, I was getting really dirty in my descrip-tions. I had the couple fucking wildly, rolling around in all different positions. Sheila stared at the TV screen as if she could actually see it too. She came again and again and again. Then, when she just couldn't come any more, she stroked me until I ex-ploded.

We lay there till the wee hours, whispering about all the different couples that we could be watching on our closed-circuit TV. Eventually we developed the idea of owning a motel of our own. In our fan-tasy motel, some of the rooms are equipped with hidden video cameras, each hooked up to a separate channel of our own television. One of us works the desk so that we can be sure that the sexiest couples are assigned to these rooms when they check in. Then we can spend the rest of the night in our room changing the channels with the remote control and watching the unsuspecting couples getting it on.

Now we play that game all the time. We talk about really going through with it one day, and we kind of pretend that we seriously might. I really don't think we'll actually come down to doing it, but it sure is fun to talk about. And it certainly has paid off in sexual dividends.

JERRY AND ELAINE

Steve:

Jerry is a judge now, but I've known him and his wife, Elaine, ever since he was a striving young lawyer with political aspirations. Although Jerry's public personality has all the dignity appropriate to his office, in private he takes pride in acting and talking like "one of the guys." One day while I was having lunch with him, he told me that he and his wife were planning a trip to the East Coast. Then he surprised me by asking, "Do you know any good sex clubs in New York City?"

He was disappointed when I explained that after living in California more than fifteen years, I probably didn't know much more about New York than he did.

"That's too bad," he said. "Elaine and I were hoping that our sex fantasy could come true in the Big Apple."

"Why don't you tell me about it?" I said, trying not to show how interested I really was. "Maybe I can make some kind of suggestion."

"Don't think you're fooling me, you sneak," Jerry said. "You're just looking for material for that book you're writing. Well, just make sure you change our names . . ."

* * *

Elaine and I have never been to New York before. But I've read that there are places there where couples go to meet other couples for group sex. Elaine and I have always been fascinated by the idea of swinging, even though we've never really gotten involved in anything like that. First of all, there's my position. Can you imagine the publicity if I ever got caught with my dick in the wrong place? And, besides, I'm not really interested in screwing any other women, and I'm especially not interested in seeing Elaine screwing any other men.

We'd both like to watch other people doing it, though. And I thought maybe you'd know a place where we could go and watch without actually getting involved ourselves. The truth is that Elaine and I have had a fantasy about that for as long as I can remember.

In our fantasy, we know of a club with an orgy room where strangers meet for mass fucking. For an extra price, we rent a private booth overlooking the orgy room. Our booth is equipped with a king-size bed and a one-way mirror so that we can see out but no one can see in. The management provides us with fine wine to help set our mood.

Sometimes we deliberately plan a night around this fantasy of ours. We dim the lights in our bedroom and get into bed, imagining that we're in our booth at the club. For a while, we sip wine, pretending that the orgy hasn't started yet. Then we take off everything we have on and lie next to each other with our eyes closed. It's very important for our eyes to be closed because that makes our fantasy more real.

We lie that way all night long, talking about what we see through the one-way glass and playing with each other. I know the kinds of scenes that turn Elaine on, and I create them for her with my imagination. She loves to hear a description of a woman getting fucked by two men at the same time. She likes me to describe their cocks and how they look entering the woman's openings.

I'll say something like, "Look at that redhead over there with the two studs. One of them has a cock as big as a baseball bat, and she's holding it tight in her hand. Look, now she's starting to suck it. Look at the way it slides into her mouth." While I'm talking, I put Elaine's hand on my cock so that, if she wants to, she can imagine that she's the woman I'm describing.

I tell her about the two men fucking the woman in the fantasy. Maybe I'll have the woman standing up and bending over so that one of them can fuck her from behind while she gives the other a blowjob. I always give them big pricks, because I know that turns Elaine on. And I always give the woman big tits because she likes it that way.

Her favorite descriptions are about a woman taking one cock in her pussy and the other up her asshole. So I try to take a while building up to that particular fantasy. First I have the woman I'm describing lick both cocks at the same time. Then I have her take one in her ass while she sucks the other. Sometimes I get really creative. I'll have the woman on her hands and knees with one man fucking her pussy while the other lies on his back under her and licks her clit.

All this time, I'm stroking and touching Elaine in all the spots that I describe to her. I put my fingers in her the way the cocks are penetrating the fantasy woman. I like to feel her excitement intensifying and increasing her wetness. When I'm sure that she's close to coming, I begin to describe the double fucking that she likes so much.

I have one of the men lying on his back on the bed with his throbbing hard-on standing up in the air. Then the woman squats over him, feeding his cock into her crack inch by inch. When it's all the way in, she lies forward, smashing her tits against his chest. As he fucks up into her, he reaches around to grab the cheeks of her ass and pull them open to show her tight asshole to the other guy.

Here, I prolong it a little by describing the way her asshole is winking open and closed above the place where a cock is sliding in and out of the drooling pussy. I tell her the guy on the bottom is sucking the woman's nipples, at the same time giving Elaine's nipples a tweak myself. At last, I describe in detail the other guy's dick and the way he positions it at the entrance to the woman's ass. He plunges slowly in until he's very deep inside her, and then the three of them begin moving in perfect rhythm, like one person.

By now, Elaine is at the brink of orgasm, so I ease up on my fingering and just concentrate on the description for a while to make it last even longer. I talk about the way it looks to see two cocks sliding in and out of her juicy holes, and I tell her how wonderful it must feel for the woman. Finally, when I think she can't stand it any longer, I start flicking her clit with my fingertip until she comes and comes and comes.

After a rest, it's my turn. I love to hear Elaine describe the sight of two women getting it on. And she does a really good job of it. She strokes my cock while she tells me how big their tits are and how their pussies look. She's especially good at detail and can go on forever with descriptions of nipples or sex lips. When she tells me that one of them is putting her mouth against the other's pussy, my dick starts to throb. She even describes the way their sex organs smell. Sometimes, while she's talking, she pushes her fingers inside herself and then holds them under my nose to give me the scent. It's so real that the fantasy almost becomes alive.

By this time I'm so excited that all I want to do is come. Elaine knows me so well that she knows just how far to push it, though. She usually manages to keep me hanging at that point for a long time by squeezing my dick or changing the description. Finally, when she decides I've had enough, she jerks me off while the women in her whispered fantasy press their mouths to each other in a steaming sixty-nine.

This sort of thing can go on all night, each of us taking turns getting the other one off. We never get tired of this game. I'm sure we'll continue playing it, no matter what we actually get to see in New York. But I am hoping that we'll get a chance to turn the fantasy into some kind of reality. Maybe if we actually find such a place, we'll chicken out. But, what the hell, at least we have our fantasy.

9   Work Out With Me

More than twenty-five years ago, President John F. Kennedy declared that Americans were among the softest people on earth. Since then, our attitudes toward physical fitness have undergone major change. Today, we are more health-conscious than we have ever been. We join health spas and racket-ball clubs. We run; we jog; we even walk circuits around shopping malls. We stretch with Richard Simmons and work out with Jane Fonda. We ride bikes, climb rocks, and swim laps. We attend weight-lifting competitions and arm-wrestling contests.

Many supermarkets are equipped with coin-operated machines to measure our pulse. For a fee, some health-food stores will determine our cholesterol count. We can even buy sphygmomanometer kits for checking our own blood pressure. We've never spent so much time thinking about our bodies.

It's natural that contemplating flesh and muscle will lead many of us to think about sex. Each time we look at the mirror to see whether we've lost a pound in the buttocks or gained an inch in the biceps, we are reminded of the pleasurable uses to which our body parts can be put. Every time we work up a sweat, we have reason to recall the fluids of coition and their scents.

When we see others exercising hard, we are likely to become aroused by the way damp garments stick to them, revealing the outlines of their genitals and breasts. Some of the togs that we wear for our workouts seem to be designed especially for erotic effect. Soft, clinging materials like spandex can make a clothed body even more intriguing to look at than a naked one.

Body culture and sensuality are so closely related that, for many people, exercise and physical fitness are the stuff that fantasies are made of. While working out, some imagine that they are having sex. While having sex, some imagine that they are working out. Others simply build their sex dreams around the dressing and undressing that accompany athletic activity.

KATY AND DAVID

Iris:

I met Katy while trying to take off a few pounds at the gym. She was an exercise instructor with a body that was the envy of all the women there. She had the figure that we were all striving to achieve. When I asked her what it would take to have a body like hers, she said that it was easy. "All you'd have to do is exercise four to six hours a day every day for the rest of your life. And having a high rate of metabolism wouldn't hurt either.''

She explained that she and her husband, David, were what most of us think of as physical-fitness nuts. They spent most of their time working on their bodies, and actually loved it. When I got to know Katy a little better, she told me about the role that physical exercise plays in their sexual fantasies. . . .

* * *

David and I have always been into physical fitness. We run together. We do gymnastics together. We lift weights together. In fact, that's how we met. We both used to go to the same gym.

A few years after we got married, we decided to have an exercise room added on to our house. One reason was that there were too many people coming to the gym who weren't really serious about their bodies. But the main reason was that we wanted to be able to work out nude together, and you can't do that at the gym.

I like to watch David's muscles flex and ripple when he lifts weights or works on the high bar. I love the way his ass gets tight and hard when he does squat lifts. There's nothing that turns me on more than looking at David's perfectly shaped body in action. I like admiring my own body too when I work out. Especially the way my breasts lift up when I flex my pecs and lacteals.

So when we had the room built, we installed mirrors throughout. Even on the ceiling. As we exercise, I find myself looking at the mirrors all the time. Sometimes I can see David's body from three or four different angles at once. It really excites me. It also excites me when I see him watching me.

There are times while he is working out that he actually gets a hard-on looking at me in the mirrors. When that happens, I start to feel my own body get all tensed up with passion. My nipples become hard, and I can see them pert and erect in the mirror. I start to move more slowly, turning the workout into an exercise in seduction instead of physical fitness.

I do deep knee-bends, real gradual, so that as I lower my body, my legs spread wide, exposing me to the mirrors. Or I bend over and touch my toes in slow motion to give David a good view of my ass.

There are times we get so turned on watching each other that we end up making love right there on the exercise mats. Then we can see ourselves in the mirror and let our imaginations go to work. We like to pretend that we're competing in the International Sexual Olympics. Maybe we're in the Freestyle Coupling event or the Rear Entry competition. We're being judged on teamwork, muscular movement, gracefulness of mating, and sexual technique.

While we make love, we look at our reflections and try to strike poses that will win us Olympic medals. I might lie flat on my back and move around until my breasts are in exactly the right position. Then David mounts me from above, turning his body so that the mirror gives us a full view of him sliding into me. David might say something like, "Listen to those cheers. The crowd loves us." Or "The judges are going to go crazy when they see your tight ass flexing that way."

Sometimes we pretend that it's the day before the

competition and we're preparing for it. We practice a particular move over and over again, trying to achieve perfection. Once, I worked on standing perfectly still with one leg extended while David, also standing, entered me from behind. My muscles got a little sore, but watching in the mirror made it worth the effort. David looked so long and hard. And when he put it in, it seemed to go deeper than ever before. I felt that we earned a gold medal for that one.

If there ever was a Sexual Olympics, David and I would be a cinch to make the U.S. team.

FRANKLIN AND CAROLINE

Steve:

A law professor's life tends to be sedentary. Sometimes it seems that the most strenuous part of the job is reshelving books after doing research. In spite of this, Franklin, a colleague who teaches at another law school, manages to keep fit. Recently, I asked what his secret was.

"Tennis," he answered. "Lots of tennis. My wife, Caroline, and I play three or four times a week. It's great for our bodies and it does wonders for our sex life too."

I was naturally curious, so I asked Franklin to explain.

"I thought that would get your interest." He chuckled. "I'll tell you about it. Maybe it'll be good enough for your book . . ."

* * *

Caroline and I have belonged to the tennis club for years. Sometimes we play doubles and sometimes just the two of us. By the time we head for the showers we've generally worked up a pretty good sweat.

I always get a kind of nostalgic sexual rush when I first step into the locker room. I guess the sight of the lockers and benches remind me of my high-school days. A schoolmate of mine once stole a key to a storeroom located next to the locker room of the school swimming pool. Using tools we borrowed from woodshop, we drilled a few peepholes in the wall. When there were girls' swimming classes, we used to sneak into the storeroom and watch the girls undress and take showers.

Those were really sexy times. I still remember them today, and the memory still turns me on. I mean, there were forty or fifty girls in there, all taking their clothes off at the same time. They were the girls we sat next to in our classes. The girls we dreamed of making it with and the girls who never let anyone touch them. There they'd be all nude and waiting for their showers, on display like a kind of visual buffet. We used to watch them for hours. Sometimes we'd masturbate while looking through the peepholes.

Anyway, one day while we were driving home from the tennis club, I told Caroline about that storeroom. I could sense right away that hearing about it was turning her on. She asked me lots of questions about how often I would go there and what I would see through the peepholes. She even asked for details about the girls we watched. What were their names? What did they look like? Did this one have big boobs? Did the redheads all have red pubic hair? That sort of thing.

By the time we got home, she was really hot. She grabbed my hand and led me right to bed. We played around for a while as we talked about that high-school locker room. Then she said she wished she could have an experience like that too. She wished she could peek into the men's locker room at the tennis club without anybody knowing it and watch the jocks getting undressed and taking showers.

Playfully, I said, "I'll tell you what. One of these days, I'll sneak you into the men's locker room, and you can hide in one of the lockers. Then you can look to your heart's content."

Caroline's breathing deepened. "Tell me," she said in a whisper. "What would I see?"

At first, I didn't know what she was getting at. "You'd see a lot of naked men," I answered.

She seemed embarrassed for a minute. Then, hesitantly, she asked, "Tell me. What would they look like?"

I didn't know quite what to say. "Well," I began. "If you'd been in there today, you would have gotten a good look at Oscar. He's got the biggest cock I've ever seen."

"How do you mean?" she asked. "Long or thick or what?"

I was flabbergasted. After all, it makes a man uncomfortable to realize that his wife is getting interested in another man's cock. But when I saw how hot it was making her, I decided to play along. I started describing Oscar's penis in detail—its length, its thickness, its color, its shape. She asked some questions that I really couldn't answer. I had never looked that closely. So I just made up the answers, giving her a real pornographic word picture. When I ran out of things to say about Oscar, she asked who else she would have seen. I gave her some lurid descriptions of other men's cocks—most of it made up.

After a while she asked about Hans, the club tennis pro. She wanted to know if he used the same locker room as the members and whether I'd ever seen him taking a shower. It was obvious that she had already done some imagining about Hans. He's a big handsome European type—German, I suppose—blond and muscular and clean-cut.

The truth was that I never had seen Hans in the shower, but Caroline was so obviously aroused that I decided to give her a treat. I went into detail about the size of his cock, telling her whatever I figured she wanted to hear. Pretending made the game more interesting.

As I spoke, she took hold of my cock and started stroking it. It felt great. I didn't want it to stop, so I really started improvising a description. Deep down, I realized that she was probably imagining that it was Hans she was stroking, but I really didn't care. What the hell, it was only make-believe.

I started stroking her too. And I kept on talking right up to the moment we both started to climax. It was like Roman candles! I know that sounds corny, but there's no other way to describe it. It was fantastic for both of us.

Since then we've played the same game on several occasions. Usually it starts while we're driving home and continues on into the bedroom and halfway through the night. Every now and then Caroline talks as though she really does plan on hiding in one of the lockers. But we both know that it's nothing more than fantasy.

RITA AND CHUCK

Iris:

Rita is a video technician who works for one of the companies that markets Steve's lectures. Sometimes, while taping, she darts around the video control room switching from one camera to another or changing video modes. Most of the time, however, she hasn't got much to do after pushing the initial button except to wait forty-five minutes for a red light to go on. During these slow sessions, she welcomes my company in the control room.

We have had many conversations during our visits. I find myself looking forward to these tapings, just for the opportunity to sit and chat with Rita. Recently, she told me about a project she and her husband, Chuck, have been working on. . . .

* * *

Chuck is an assistant producer with a TV station. He and I have a great idea for a unique exercise video. It could be a best-seller. Hotter than "Jane Fonda's Workout."

We're both into aerobics and have seen every exercise tape on the market. Some are so easy that it's no fun to work out with them. Others are so hard that you'd have to be a professional athlete to keep up. Our idea is for a workout that would be challenging for everyone, but not impossible for anyone. It should also be so much fun that nobody would look for an excuse to put it off. Most important, it should be something that would sell like crazy.

Of course, there's only one thing that can do all that. Sex! So we are going to call it Sexercises. The trick is to come up with sexual positions that will exercise all the muscles of the body as well as stimulate the sexual appetite. Couples can work out together to improve not only their bodies but their sex lives as well.

Every time we make love, we work on parts of our Sexercises routine. Naturally, we plan on being the demonstrators on the tape. We haven't finished putting the routine together yet, but we have come up with a few exercises for it.

We begin with jumping jacks as a warmup. For the rest of the routine, we will be completely nude, but it isn't advisable to do jumping exercises without some support. So Chuck wears a jockstrap and I wear an exercise bra. I like looking at the outline of Chuck's balls inside his jock. He always has his eyes glued to my boobs watching them bob up and down. At this point, the camera should zoom in for close-ups to show the outline of my nipples against the bra and the way Chuck fills out his jock.

When we're both perspiring heavily, we take off what we're wearing. By now, there's a river of sweat flowing between my breasts, and Chuck's cock is glistening with moisture. The camera zooms in on this too.

Now we're ready for the next Sexercise. We each lie head-to-foot on our left side and raise our right leg. In this position, Chuck can look right into my pussy as it opens with the leg lifts. And I can watch his cock and balls move as his muscles tense. I like the way his testicles shift with the movements of his leg.

Of course, the idea is for the viewers to get turned on watching us so that they will turn on to each other. So here again the camera zooms in for close-ups to show just what each of us is seeing. First it focuses on my crotch, so that the viewer can see me open and close while watching the movement of my legs. Then it zooms in on Chuck, who usually is erect by this time.

We do twenty of these on each side before moving on to our back-to-back stand-ups. These are good for tightening up the thighs and hips. First we sit back-to-back on the floor and just push against each other. I always get excited feeling Chuck's powerful back muscles flexing. Then we interlock our elbows and work our way up to a standing position by pressing our backs together and taking little backward steps with our feet. When we are both standing erect, our asses are pushed together and I can feel the firmness of his buttocks against mine. We work our way down and up again until we have done ten of these.

Now we're ready for my favorite. This one takes good timing and coordination, but it's worth it. Chuck lies on his back with his hands clasped behind his head and does sit-ups. I stand straddling him, my back to his face and feet on either side of his waist, and do ankle touches. We time our movements so that when I am bent over and grasping my ankles, Chuck is sitting upright with his face against my crotch. He mouths me for a moment while I look back between my legs at his rigid cock. Then I stand up and he lies back again. We are up to thirty repetitions.

Another great Sexercise that we've come up with combines leg raises and push-ups. I lie on my back with my legs spread into a V-shape. Then, without bending my knees, I lift my legs slowly into the air. Chuck does push-ups on the floor between my legs. When he comes down, my legs are up and spread wide apart, his face within inches of my open vulva. The camera should come in close to show the viewer exactly what Chuck is seeing when I'm in the different leg-raise poses. No man in his right mind would skip his push-ups if he could do them in this position.

After each of us does ten, the exercise gets even more stimulating. Chuck crawls forward until he is on top of me and his erection is buried deep inside of me. Here again, the camera can focus on the sexual action. Chuck continues doing push-ups while I hold my legs in a vertical position, opening and closing them around his waist. Most men would be very close to climax at this point, but the physical strain of push-ups can help put off their orgasm. You might call this an exercise in control.

We've also developed a special variation on knee bends for the woman who wants to change excess flab into muscle on her thighs and hips. Chuck lies on his back arching his body so that all his weight is supported by his heels and the back of his head. Facing him, I squat over his penis and slide it slowly into me. Then, just using the muscles of my thighs, I lift myself up until only the head of it remains inside. I move my hips in a circle and then lower myself again until I am practically sitting on him.

Chuck just loves this one, because it opens me up and allows him to see every detail of the penetration. The camera focuses on our merging genitals as we grind away. The great thing about it is that the sensations always drive me on to two or three more repetitions, even after I've done my twenty. The first time I tried it, I really ached the next day. But you know the expression: no pain, no gain.

Another one of our Sexercises is based on a yoga posture. It stretches almost every muscle of the body. I begin by lying on my back. Then I lift myself up onto my neck, shoulders, and elbows to get into the bicycle position. After pedaling my feet in the air, I lower my knees to the floor on each side of my head. This puts my buttocks and vulva into the utmost open position. It's Chuck's finale.

From a standing position, he bends his knees, supporting his weight with the muscles of his calves and thighs until his erection is level with my opening. After he inserts himself, he thrusts in and out while keeping his back perfectly straight. The camera gets an excellent view of Chuck's tightly muscled ass flexing. And it's a great opportunity to give the viewers a bonus by zeroing in on the insertion and following Chuck's big dick as it slides in and out of me. Twenty in-and-outs would be ideal, but I bet lots of people would come before they got that far. I know we usually do.

If we ever actually did make a tape like this, I'll bet it would be a really big seller. Chances are we never will. But that doesn't matter. Fantasizing about it has already paid off in dividends.

10 We're Being Watched

The desire to show one's genitals off to other people is known as exhibitionism. Carried to extremes, psychiatrists think of exhibitionism as a mental disease, and courts treat it as a crime. People who take their clothes off in public may be convicted of indecent exposure, public lewdness or disturbing the peace.

Women are almost never prosecuted for these offenses. Probably this is because, until recently, most of the people who made and enforced our laws were men. Since most men—even cops and legislators—like looking at naked women, they haven't seen any reason to lock women up for undressing publicly. But a recent study found that about one in nine of the men doing time for sex crimes had been convicted of engaging in some form of exhibitionism. A Stanford University textbook points out ironically that if a man watches a woman undressing in front of an open window, he is called a Peeping Tom, but if they change places, he is called an exhibitionist.

Most students of human behavior agree that the kicks that accompany exhibitionism begin early in childhood. Children usually discover and handle their own genitals before they are six, some when they are only three. After they begin fondling themselves, they often feel a need to demonstrate their discovery to others. For this reason, exhibitionism is the most common form of childhood sex play outside of masturbation itself.

Since our society provides adults with few legitimate outlets for public nudity, our exhibitionism becomes more subtle as we grow older. Most of the time, we indulge the desire to show off our sexual parts by wearing clothes that hint at but do not actually reveal them. Unbuttoned shirts, see-through blouses, brief shorts, hip-hugging pants, and denim jeans are all designed to accentuate those areas of the body that we think of as erotic—the chest, the breasts, the buttocks, and the crotch.

Since the satisfaction that comes from this kind of symbolic display is somewhat limited, it is easy to understand why so many sexually successful couples make exhibitionism an important part of their fantasies. For some, the whispered scenarios are completely imaginary. They simply invent an audience to watch them in their erotic play. Others base their exhibitionist fantasies on events that actually happened to them. They exaggerate and elaborate as they recall a particular incident in which they were, or could have been, observed in a state of undress or in the process of having sex.

In a way, exhibitionism was at work every time we interviewed a couple about their favorite fantasy. Even those whose fantasies are described in other chapters of this book were indulging some form of exhibitionist drive when they told us about their sexual activities. By doing so, they were making us, and you, the audience to their eroticism.

MARILYN AND JOHN

Iris:

Marilyn and John are in their early thirties and have been living together for the past eight years. According to Marilyn, ''We'll probably get married someday, but so far, we just haven't gotten around to it.'' John is employed by a large supermarket chain as a district purchasing manager. Marilyn owns a hairstyle and manicure studio with nine employees. She used to cut hair, but now spends all of her professional time supervising her employees and managing the studio.

As a customer in Marilyn's studio for several years, I occasionally had frank conversations with her about sex. She knew that Steve and I had written sex books, and often kidded me by calling me ''oversexed Iris.'' During one of our conversations, Marilyn said that she and John like to play fantasy games in bed. I could tell by the way she looked at me that she wanted me to ask what she meant, so I did. Her answer was, ''We talk about things while we screw.''

I think I said something like, ''Yes, we do too,'' but neither of us said much more about it at the time. Months later, though, I told Marilyn that we were gathering material for this book and asked if she and John would be willing to talk to us about their fantasy games. Marilyn jumped at the chance. "We'd love to," she said.

"Don't you want to ask John first?" I asked, laughing.

But Marilyn just winked and flashed an impish smile. "Trust me," she said. "He'll love it." She promised that she and John would meet with us that very night.

During the interview, Marilyn did all of the talking. Since she knew me and had met Steve a few times, this may have been because she was more comfortable than John, who had never met either of us. But Steve and I both got the impression that Marilyn did most of the talking in bed, too. . . .

* * *

We don't usually do it until we're in bed together nude and we've already been fooling around for a while. Then, all I have to say is, "He's watching us," and I can immediately feel John's cock jump. He likes it when I talk about our imaginary audience.

I don't really remember how it started, but we've always gotten off on the idea of fucking while another man is in the room watching us. We don't have any particular man in mind. Nobody we know. Just a man. He doesn't say anything. He just stands there naked, playing with his cock while he watches us.

We build up slowly, stroking each other, licking each other. John really likes to play with my boobs. And I like it too. Every now and then while he's doing it, I tell him about the man in the room. I say, "He can't take his eyes off what you're doing," or "He's staring at my tits."

Then, as we go on to other things, I keep up the report. "He's watching you put your finger in my pussy."

It's funny. John is very jealous. When we're out together, he gets angry if he thinks that some other man is even looking at me. But in our fantasy game, he loves the idea. Sometimes I ask him to show me to the other man, and he pretends to do it. I'll say, "Hold up my tits so he can see them." And John will cup them and hold them up. Or I'll say, "Open my pussy so he can look inside." And John does it. When I feel John spreading me with his fingers, I close my eyes and I imagine that a strange man is really watching and jerking off.

When I tell John that, he usually asks me to describe the guy's cock. We watch a lot of porno, so I've seen a lot of cocks. I keep my eyes closed and try to imagine one of the cocks I've seen. Then, when I have a real good picture of it in my mind, I describe it. It's better if it's different each time. Sometimes it's long and fat, with a throbbing purple head. Sometimes it's curved, or pointed. Sometimes I describe the drops of moisture oozing out of its tip.

When we get to this point, we're usually ready to start fucking. As John slides into me, I talk about the way the guy is masturbating. "He's squeezing the shaft now. Real tight. He loves the way you're fucking me."

By that time, I'm so hot that I forget about the fantasy. All I can do is concentrate on my own orgasm. And John's.

DEBBIE AND SAL

Iris:

My friend Debbie lived on the same street as I did when we were growing up in Manhattan. She was four years older than I and was my idol. Even as a teenager, she was recognized by all who knew her as an exceptional beauty, with long dark hair and sparkling blue eyes. She had the figure of a movie star, and to me, she was even sexier than Marilyn Monroe. She spoke in a husky voice that dripped with sex, her movements were fluid and erotic, and she knew things that I hadn't even begun to dream about.

Debbie married at the age of eighteen when I was an impressionable girl of fourteen. Since my mother was always too embarrassed to talk with me about sex, Debbie became my authority. She told me that There was nothing dirty about sex, insisting that it was a beautiful experience. I've always been grateful to Debbie for passing her healthy attitudes along to me.

When Steve and I published our first adult novel, Debbie was the first to congratulate us on our literary achievement. Afterward, she referred to me proudly as her protégé. Naturally, when I told her that we were writing a book about couples' fantasies, she insisted on being part of it. We chatted over coffee about several fantasy games that have kept her marriage to Sal young and full of excitement for almost thirty years. We chose to include this particular one because Debbie says that it is her favorite. . . .

* * *

Sal's work takes us out of town every now and then, and there's nothing I like better than staying at a hotel. Probably, that's because when Sal and I were first going out together, we spent many evenings in hotel rooms making love. To this day, every time we check into a hotel or motel, I find myself getting wet in the pants.

Usually, when we spend a night in a hotel, Sal and I fantasize that people in the adjoining rooms can see us even though we can't see them. We imagine that all the mirrors in our room are one-way mirrors and that the walls and ceiling are dotted with peepholes. We pretend that the people who are watching us all came to the motel to have sex, like we did before we were married, and that they found the peepholes by accident.

From the minute we get into the room, we know we are being watched. I start performing immediately. Even while I'm unpacking, I try to put on a show for my unseen audience. I strip down to my slip and find a reason to walk around for a while before I open the suitcase. I love the feel of all those imaginary eyes on me.

Sal knows me well enough to know when my exhibition show has begun. He watches me for a while and then pulls the slip off over my head. Sometimes we stand in the middle of the room and he puts his hands on my shoulders, turning me around so that everybody can see me in my bra and panties. I always wear sexy underwear when traveling.

I talk to him about the audience while we're hanging up our clothes. "Do you think I look all right? Do you think they'll like my body?"

Sal goes right along with it. "How could they not?"

He brings me in front of a mirror and unhooks my bra while standing behind me. I like looking in the mirror as he slips it off to uncover my breasts and cup them in his hands. I always get a little excited looking at my own breasts, but when I think of all those eyes lurking behind the mirror, I get even more excited. I love watching my nipples get hard and then showing them to the audience.

I gyrate my pelvis, rubbing my buttocks against the front of Sal's pants so I can feel his hard-on against me. I reach back and undo his belt, and watch in the mirror as his pants fall to his feet. Sal never wears underwear, you know, so his cock springs right out as soon as his pants are down. I like to imagine that there are lots of women looking at him, but of course I'm the only one who gets him.

Sometimes, I take Sal in my mouth. He says that I'm great at giving head, and I want all the people who are watching us to see me do it. I love to get down on my knees and suck him while he stands there. I especially like when he groans in pleasure because I know that this must be very entertaining for our audience. I can almost hear their sighs.

After a while, I lie back on the bed and let Sal remove my panties. By this time, I'm usually so wet that the crotch part sticks to me. I like the way it feels when it clings for that extra second. And then I'm nude. I feel my pussy flowering open because of the attention I'm getting from the people looking through the peepholes. When I look up at the ceiling, I can imagine a couple in the room above us staring down at my clit. It swells so big that I can feel it separating the lips that surround it.

Sal starts licking me, running his tongue up and down my slit, shoving it inside and then caressing the outside. He makes his tongue long and stiff like a cock and fucks me with it while I hold my pussy open with my fingers so that everybody can see. I feel so vulnerable lying back like that with my legs spread open while they watch Sal eat me. I feel like I can come within seconds.

Most of the time, I get up off the bed before I come. I stand in front of the dresser, looking into the mirror and trying to picture what the people on the other side of it look like. I arch my body forward thrusting my breasts toward them. In a loud voice so that everyone will hear, I tell Sal to put his cock into me. Then I groan and gasp so that everyone will know how good it feels for me.

All eyes are on us as we pump against each other. By now I'm so excited that I come almost immediately. The second I start, Sal comes too. No matter how intense the orgasm is, though, we never forget our audience.

ROLFE AND CLAUDIA

Steve:

Rolfe is one of those hard-to-find auto mechanics who fixes it right the first time he works on it. He's been servicing our cars for as long as I care to remember. Several years ago, Rolfe told me that he and his wife, Susan, were not getting along and asked if I could give him some legal advice. I told him that I wasn't actively practicing law or representing clients, but I offered to listen.

Rolfe began by calling his marriage to Susan a "sexual disaster" and saying that it had been that way right from the start. He claimed that he and Susan did not even have intercourse until after they had been married for two weeks, and that after that it had never been satisfying for either of them. The problem, he said, was that Susan did not have "a healthy interest in sex." For example, he said that she had never once during the course of their marriage performed oral sex on him or permitted him to perform it on her. She thought that the missionary position (she called it the "normal position") was the only way to have intercourse that was not disgusting, and most of the time she wasn't particularly interested in having intercourse at all. He said that she wouldn't let him come into the bathroom when she was bathing and that he couldn't remember ever seeing her completely nude.

Rolfe confessed that he had been having an affair with Claudia, a woman who had been sent by a temporary-employment agency to handle some of his shop's typing needs. He said that he had found sexual happiness with Claudia and wanted to divorce Susan so that he and Claudia could get married. I told him a little about the state's divorce laws and recommended an attorney.

During the months that followed, I learned that Susan was being uncooperative, bitterly resisting Rolfe's attempt to be free of her. Three years ago, however, he succeeded in obtaining a divorce and married Claudia the very next day.

Recently, when I told Rolfe that Iris and I were writing a book about couples' sexual fantasies, he said, "You ought to include mine and Claudia's. Sometimes I think it's the only thing that stopped us from committing murder. . . ."

* * *

When I was trying to get the divorce, Susan made my life so miserable that I wanted to kill her. My lawyer said that there was no way she could prevent me from getting the divorce, but that she could delay it. And she certainly did. She fought me every step of the way. When I said that I wanted to keep the house, she said that she wanted it. Then, when I offered to give it to her, she said that she couldn't afford to keep it up. Finally we had to sell it and divide up the money.

Claudia worked as a temporary for a different company every day. But Susan used to find out where Claudia was working and call her up on the phone to say nasty things. Sometimes she'd even manage to talk to whoever Claudia was working for and bad-mouth her. Most of the time the boss would figure out what was going on and ignore it, but Susan did cause her to lose a couple of jobs.

Claudia and I used to spend a lot of time talking about the things we'd like to do to Susan. Never serious, you understand. But we'd say things like we were going to get a Mafia hit man to knock her off, or we were going to drop a bomb on her house, or stuff like that. Then one night Claudia got this brilliant idea. What we really ought to do, she said, is force Susan to see what a good time we have when we make love. We ought to make her watch us do something that would really horrify her. We ought to make her watch my cock sliding into Claudia's ass.

I'll never forget that night. Sex with Claudia has always been great. But that night set a new standard.

First we talked about Susan being tied to a chair in a corner of the room. Then Claudia took off everything she was wearing except her panties and got onto the bed on her hands and knees. She bent forward until her shoulders were touching the bed and waved her ass high in the air. Then she said, "Here, Susan. Watch while Rolfe takes off my panties."

At first I felt a little silly playing pretend games. But as I slid Claudia's panties off, I got so excited that I forgot to feel silly. Her panties were pink and soft. They were the short kind that just barely cover anything anyway. I tugged at them slowly, exposing her smooth white ass, and rolled them down and slipped them off. By then, I could almost visualize Susan watching, and I was starting to get into the game.

I held the panties up to my nose and inhaled deeply. I knew that it would embarrass the shit out of Susan, and the thought was really turning me on. Claudia was getting off on it too, so I said, "Oh, Susan, Claudia's panties are all wet with the juices from her pussy. They smell so good. Your panties never smelled like this."

When I said it, I heard Claudia sigh. We both imagined Susan sitting there watching with a shocked expression on her face and squirming in humiliation. From then on, the idea was to do things we knew would upset Susan.

I started by kissing the cheeks of Claudia's ass. She rocked backward, forcing them apart and exposing the crack between them. I had never done anything like this before, but the idea of upsetting Susan made it easy. I began licking her anus. I was surprised at how good it felt. I think Claudia was surprised, too, when I started to do it, because I heard her gasp.

But a minute later she got right into it. "Oh, that feels good," she said. "I bet he never did anything like this to you, Susan. You know why he's licking me there? He's getting me all wet so he can fuck me in the ass. Bet you never got fucked in the ass."

I really wasn't planning to do that, but I got carried away with the idea of putting on a show for ,Susan. So I got onto my knees behind Claudia's ass and began pressing the tip of my dick into that crack between her cheeks. I still don't think I was actually planning to put it in. But I could feel her crack spreading open and the head of my cock pushing its way inside.

Claudia's body was moving forward and back. Each time she rocked back, she pressed her ass against my thrust, forcing me in deeper. Suddenly, I realized that I was buried all the way in her belly. The sounds of Claudia's moans were driving me crazy, and for a moment I forgot all about Susan. Then Claudia said, "Do you see that, you bitch? He's fucking me in the ass. And I love every second of it."

We threw ourselves against each other like two

animals, puffing and panting as I drove deeper and deeper into her. Sometimes I swear I could actually see Susan sitting there with a look of horror on her face. It felt so good, I thought I had died and gone to heaven.

"Faster, harder," Claudia was moaning. "Oh, Rolfie, it feels wonderful."

I felt like I was going to explode, but I didn't want it to end. So I stopped moving for a minute and just poised there with my cock halfway inside her. I reached around with one hand and began to stroke her pussy very lightly. Then, because I knew it would excite Claudia even more, I said, "Susan, can you see me touching Claudia's sweet sex? Her clit is as hard as a rock and so big I can feel it throb. Your clit never got this big, Susan. I don't even think you have one."

Claudia began to make noises I had never heard her make before. And I could feel her pussy oozing with wetness. I held up my hand and said, "Look at this juice, Susan. It tastes so sweet." I licked my fingers loud, making slurping sounds for Claudia to hear. I could picture Susan's shocked face as I rubbed my wet fingertips over the exposed part of my cock. The thought of Susan watching made my hips start pushing again, and I drove deeper into Claudia's ass while reaching again for her clit.

"Oh, God," Claudia moaned. "I'm going to come any second. Come with me, Rolfe. Come with me so that Susan can see us both come at the same time."

"Yes," I shouted. "I'm coming. I'm coming now."

That was all it took to get Claudia started. Her asshole squeezed tight around my cock as her contractions began. I knew that she was having an orgasm even before she said it. "Me, too. I'm coming with you."

Somehow, that orgasm seemed to last forever. Then, when it was finished for both of us, we just stayed that way, with my cock up her ass for a long time. I think we did it three more times that same night.

In a way, that night changed our sex life. Ever since then, we've known the trick of how to turn each other on. We don't do it that way every time, but whenever we want something special, we tie Susan to that chair and make her watch while I fuck Claudia in the ass. It's gotten to the point where all one of has to do is say, "Susan," when we're talking on the phone or something and it keeps both of us hot for the rest of the day. 'Cause we know that night it's going to be like that first time all over again.

I don't hate Susan anymore. Why should I? She's helped to give me some of the best sex I've ever had. Even if she doesn't know it.

11 Lights, Camera, Action!

Some people claim that they can tell a man's age by the way he reacts to the sight of a woman's undergarment. They point to generations of male adolescents who discovered the pleasures of masturbation while studying advertisements for ladies' underwear in mail-order catalogs. Prior to 1957, they add, these were the most erotic pictures legitimately available in the United States.

Until that year, all states had laws that strictly prohibited the publication of photographs depicting nude human bodies. Then the U.S. Supreme Court changed everything by deciding the case of *Roth v. United States*. Roth had been convicted of violating a state law that prohibited the sale of obscene material. He appealed his conviction to the Supreme Court, claiming that the law violated his right to freedom of expression under the First Amendment to the Constitution.

The Supreme Court stated that material could not be called obscene merely because it depicted nude bodies or described sexual intercourse. The Court defined obscenity in a way that permitted the sale of books and films that, until then, could only have been obtained or produced clandestinely. According to the new definition, nothing was obscene unless it appealed primarily to an unnatural interest in sex, was offensive under contemporary community standards, and was utterly without redeeming social value.

It was this last requirement that opened the doors to legal pornography. Nearly everything can be said to have some social value. As one of our publishers put it when we were writing adult fiction, "You can fill the book with all the fucking and sucking you want, as long as one of the characters tells the reader to buy U.S. savings bonds."

Soon after the *Roth* decision, film producers began to realize that they could get away with almost anything. Before long, neighborhood theaters were showing films like *I Am Curious* and *Deep Throat.* With improvements in technology, pornographic movies on videotape became available to every middle-class American household.

In 1973, the Supreme Court retreated from its ultra-permissive definition. In the case of *Miller v. California,* the justices said that a work doesn't have to be *utterly* without value to be obscene if, taken as a whole, it lacks serious literary, artistic, political, or scientific merit. Obviously, this change did little to affect the availability of explicit erotic material.

Today, X-rated videotapes can be purchased or rented in almost every city in the United States. As a result, many couples have made this form of erotica an integral part of their sex lives. Some simply watch porno together, letting it increase their own sexual desire. Others weave the pornography into their shared fantasies. They pretend to have sex with characters in the films they see, or even pretend that they are the stars of those films. A few actually produce their own private pornography, using inexpensive video cameras to turn their fantasies into reality.

SHERRY AND TED

Iris:

Sherry and Ted own a video shop where Steve and I often rent movies. They are a quiet couple in their mid-fifties. Sherry has gray hair that she keeps in a rather severe-looking bun. Ted is on the paunchy side, with a mild paternal smile.

They look so conservative that when we wanted to rent porno movies, Steve and I always used to go to a different shop. Once, however, I noticed a black loose-leaf book on their counter and asked Sherry what it was. She looked around carefully before answering. Then, in a lowered voice, she said, "That's a list of our adult titles. We don't keep them out on the shelves where kids could see them, but we have quite a selection."

Surprised, I began leafing through the book. It turned out that they had the most complete collection of X-rated videos that we had seen. We began renting porno movies from them. At first, we were slightly embarrassed about it, but Sherry's attitude was so matter-of-fact that our embarrassment soon faded.

One day, knowing that Steve is a law professor, Ted asked if Steve thought that he could get into any kind of trouble for renting porno movies. Since this area of the law is a favorite of his, Steve proceeded to give Ted and Sherry a ten-minute course on constitutional law and the regulation of obscenity. From that point on, the shopkeepers treated us more as friends than as customers.

Sherry began giving me a little critique of each porno film that we asked about renting. It was evident that she and Ted had seen them all, some several times. She spoke about the movies frankly, describing scenes with a candor inconsistent with her conservative appearance.

One day, in her straightforward manner, she told me that she and Ted liked to play sex games while they watched X-rated movies. I tried hard to cover my incredulity, but didn't succeed. "Really?" I asked. "What kind of games?"

Sherry's answer reminded me of a lesson that I've learned hundreds of times, but that I still manage to forget where sex is concerned: You really can't judge a book by its cover.

* * *

Ted and I met in church and we've always been active in church affairs. But that doesn't mean that we don't have an exciting sex life. We both believe that God made sex along with everything else in the universe, and that all of God's creations are beautiful. Ted and I have been married for more than thirty years, and we still make love three or four times a week.

Whenever we get a new movie, we take it home and watch it, including the adult titles. If we're watching one of those and it's any good at all, we usually can't get through it without having sex ourselves. Ted loves to talk while we watch. I call it talking dirty. He tells me what scenes he likes and how he would improve them if he were directing the movie. I always say that Ted missed his calling. He's got such an erotic imagination he should be in the porno industry himself. I'm only kidding, of course, but you'd be surprised if you heard some of his ideas.

The best thing is when he puts me in the movie. What I mean is that sometimes, when something really exciting is happening to one of the girls on the screen, he says that it's me. If a cute blonde is having anal sex with a man with a tremendous johnny, Ted'll say, "Can you feel that big thing in you? Doesn't it feel good?" Things like that.

When there's a close-up of a man's penis, he tells me to look at it because it's going to be inside me in a minute. Then, when it starts to slide into some little porno queen, he describes how it's going into me. Ted is the only man I've every known, and the only man I'd ever really want to go to bed with. But I get very excited when he pairs me up with those hot young studs on the screen.

His words make it seem so real that I stare at the TV in a trance, really experiencing sex with whatever male sex star is in the movie. Most of the time, Ted doesn't touch me at all while he's talking dirty. He just stimulates my imagination and lets me fantasize about making it with the horny young man. Sometimes he makes me so hot with his words that I feel my underpants getting all wet in the crotch. I tell Ted when that happens, and it always turns him on. I think if I let him go on talking, I could have a climax without ever being touched. But by then I want to feel him and I ask him to make love to me.

Somehow I know that making love to Ted is better than it could ever be with one of those X-rated studs. But it sure is fun to dream about it.

BRIAN AND ANN

Steve:

For a few years, I taught an undergraduate course called Law and Society at a university in Southern California. Most of the class material was concerned with the way the U.S. Constitution protects individual rights. One topic that always aroused the interests of the students was the constitutional protection of pornography. Some felt that the law was too permissive and that it encouraged a decline in morality. Others argued that the law was not protective enough, and that all restrictions on freedom of expression paved the way to fascism. No one was indifferent. The subject sparked even those who were usually nonparticipators.

Brian, a military careerist around my age, was a student who did not ordinarily speak out in class. But he was absolutely eloquent in his defense of pornography. He argued passionately during class and talked to me at great length about the subject afterward. While we were having a cup of coffee together in the school cafeteria, he said, "Pornography is a very healthy influence. It's certainly done wonders for my girlfriend and me. . . ."

* * *

Ann and I have been living together for eighteen years. We have a real good thing going, but it hasn't always been roses. There was a time about six years ago when it looked like we were going to break up. We weren't fighting or anything like that. We just sort of seemed to be bored with each other, especially in bed.

We tried a lot of things to improve our sex life. We read some of those books about sexual technique. Ann tried to plan romantic suppers. We even talked to a counselor at the base. Then one night, I rented an X-rated video, hoping that it might help get us turned on.

Well, it worked. Watching the movie got us both so aroused that by the time it ended, we were making really passionate love. We both fell asleep exhausted. Over breakfast the next day we talked about the film and got ourselves all worked up again. It was the first time in years that we had sex in the morning.

After that, I started bringing home X-rated movies regularly. We'd watch them in bed and make wonderful love. Sometimes, we'd critique the performances of the actors and actresses. That's how we got started on our little game.

We were watching a woman go down on a man

when Ann said, "The camera's not in the right place. If I were directing this picture, I'd move in for a close-up of her tongue going up and down on his shaft. And I'd have her open her mouth every once in a while and take his whole head inside it."

Ann's words got to me. I enjoyed hearing her talk that way, and I liked the fantasy of directing a porno flick. So I got into it with her. "And I'd tell her to lick the rest of him, too," I said. "And pay a little more attention to his balls. Don't you think so?"

"Yes," Ann answered. "I'd have her do it just like this." With that, she bent over me and started licking the insides of my thighs, working her way slowly but definitely up toward my balls. I could feel the warm breath from her mouth washing over my scrotum as she kissed them gently.

I looked at the screen again and said, "And now I'd tell her to work on his shaft."

Ann responded by flicking her tongue over my penis from the base to the head. She had never done anything like that before. I wouldn't say that she had been opposed to oral sex, but it wasn't one of her specialties. Now, though, she was doing it like a champ.

The characters in the porno film had changed positions. The woman was leaning back with her legs spread and the man was licking her vagina. Glancing at the screen, I asked Ann what she thought of that.

"He should go more slowly," she said. "First he should tongue the outside lips real lightly. Then he should slip it slowly inside her." As she spoke, Ann lay back and opened her thighs. Placing her hands on my head, she guided my face down to her puckering vulva. "He's got to be gentle."

I started lapping and nibbling at her, trying to follow the directions she was giving to the actor on the screen. I never knew her to enjoy it so much before. As I eased my tongue into her opening, she sighed. I could taste the juices welling up inside her.

"Now he should lick the clitoris," she whispered. "Using just the tip of his tongue."

I got the idea immediately and began lapping lightly at her little love button. I could hear her moan, "Oh, God, this feels so good." She said it over and over again as I teased gently at the tiny pressure point. I could feel it getting larger and larger. And at the same time harder and harder. I couldn't ever remember it being so big and swollen before.

"I'm going to come," she wailed. "If you don't stop soon, I'm going to come." Her hips kept thrusting at my mouth. Maybe she thought that she wanted me to stop, but her body didn't agree. Her pelvis lifted up against me as her womb cried out for more. I could taste juices oozing from her crack and bathing her clit.

"Now," she shouted. "I'm coming now." It was the first time she ever came in my mouth, and so fast I couldn't believe it. There had been times when I was sure she was faking it, but there was no doubt that this was the real thing. I kept thrashing her lightly with my tongue, enjoying the wonderful sounds of her pleasure until her climax was over and she just lay there purring quietly.

After a while, we started talking about the movie

again. We ended up doing some more great things for the first time. It was the best night either of us ever had.

We've learned a lot about each other's sexual needs since then. It seems that until that night neither of us really knew what the other liked or wanted. And we were too embarrassed to talk openly about it. Maybe we both thought it would seem like we were being too demanding. But when we were watching pornos, we were able to express our hidden desires by pretending to be directing the action on the screen.

We still watch X-rated movies from time to time, but we've become so open about our needs that we feel free to use our imaginations even when we're not watching them. You might say that imagination saved our relationship.

JONI AND SAM

Iris:

Joni and Sam are neighbors of ours. Sometimes, Steve and I can see them sunbathing on their patio without clothes or cavorting nude in their swimming pool and spa. Once, when I tried to tell Joni that her hedges weren't giving her as much privacy as she thought, she just laughed.

"We know we can be seen," she said. "We don't mind. In fact, we like the idea. Someday Sam and I are going to audition for parts in a porno movie."

"Oh, really?" I asked, a little surprised.

"Well, probably not really," she admitted reluctantly. "But we sure have a lot of fun rehearsing in front of our video camera. . . ."

* * *

Sam and I used to rent lots of porno movies to play on our VCR. They used to get us so horny that we'd start screwing in the middle, and half the time we never even got to see the end. One night we were watching one on the TV and watching ourselves in the bedroom mirror at the same time, when Sam said, "We're better than the people in that movie. We ought to become porno stars ourselves."

The next day, Sam came home with a new toy—a video camera. He set it up on a tripod in our bedroom and said, "Joni, this is your screen test. If you want a part in my next porno movie, show me what you can do."

The idea of auditioning for a porno-movie director really appealed to me. "Let's get a little background music," I suggested. I went to the record cabinet and picked out a record called *The Stripper*. It's one of my favorites. Sam says he's seen dancers strip to it in burlesque shows, and I've never been able to listen to it without picturing myself as a stripper on the stage.

As the music started, I found myself getting all excited. The camera was pointed at me, and I could see myself on the TV screen. I began swaying to the music, working my way into the rhythm. After dancing a little, I started unbuttoning my blouse, trying to make my movements as sexy as possible.

When my top was completely unbuttoned, I pulled

it open to reveal my lacy bra and then quickly pulled it shut again, like I imagined a burlesque queen would do. Turning my back to the camera, I slowly slipped the blouse downward to expose my bare shoulders. When my entire back was uncovered, I dropped the blouse to the floor and turned to face the camera again.

An inch at a time, I lifted the hem of my skirt until it was almost up to my crotch, and then let it drop. Slowly, I teased the zipper of my skirt up and down. Finally, I removed it completely.

Wearing nothing but my bra and panty hose, I began dancing in front of the camera, rocking my hips back and forth in a series of bumps and grinds. I glanced at Sam to see his reaction. He was enjoying himself, staring at me through wide eyes. I looked at the TV screen. My pubic hair was a dark shadowy patch showing through the crotch of the sheer hose. I rubbed my mound with the palm of my hand and then hooked my thumbs into the waistband.

With slow and deliberate movements, I stripped the panty hose over my hips and down to my ankles, completely exposing my pussy. I felt naughty and daring as I picked up the nylons with my toes and kicked them toward the camera. Quickly, I turned and wiggled my backside, shaking my buttocks wantonly.

Spreading my legs, I bent forward and looked up at the camera from between my thighs. I waved to Sam as he focused the camera on my naked ass. I could see the dark crease of my anus winking at me from the TV screen.

I stood again and unhooked my bra with my back

to the camera. Pirouetting slowly, I brought my tits into full view. I could see that Sam was really excited watching me; his hard-on made that obvious. But to tell the truth, I think I was even more excited than he was. I shook my shoulders, making my tits bounce and roll from side to side. Sam always says that I've got tits as big as footballs, and on the TV screen they looked even bigger.

My nipples were bright red, with thick points that were as hard as rubies. I cupped my tits with my hands, forcing the nipples to jut out from between my fingers. Lifting my breasts one at a time, I licked my nipples until they were covered with a layer of glistening saliva. This made them bigger than ever. I was putting on a show for Sam and the camera, but I was also doing it because it felt so good. My vagina felt like it was on fire.

"Okay, now," Sam said. "Let's see you do something really dirty. How about spreading your legs wide and playing with your pussy."

I didn't need any more encouragement than that. Watching myself on the TV screen, I threw myself back on the bed and parted my thighs as far as they could go. Sam made the camera zoom in for a close-up of my crotch. I could see droplets of moisture dotting the pink membranes of my labia. And my clit was standing up proud and tall.

I framed my slit with the fingers of one hand while I stroked it with the other. The camera followed every move. Spreading the lips apart, I inserted one finger into my opening as deep as it would go. It felt so good that my clit started to throb. Raising my hand to my mouth, I licked the juices off my finger and winked into the camera. I felt wanton, like a porno queen. I could hear Sam's breathing deepen.

I stuffed two fingers into my pussy, and then three. Slowly, I moved them in and out, trying to imitate the movements that Sam's cock makes when he's fucking me. At the same time, I started stroking my clit with my thumb. My entire vaginal opening was covered with the fluid that oozed from my pouting slit.

I felt a climax building and watched the TV screen intently as I churned away at my pussy. What I saw was hotter than any porno movie we had ever rented. The tissues of my inner lips were bright rosy pink. As I plunged in and out, the sex flesh clung to my fingers, turning in as I drove them deeper and turning out as I withdrew them. I heard moaning sounds coming from the TV and realized that I was making them.

"Oooh, this feels soooo good," I practically sang. "I'm so I hot I'm going to come any second." My words were exciting me as much as they were exciting Sam. I humped harder and faster as I reached for orgasm with every fiber of my body.

Sam made a guttural sound that caused me to tear my eyes from the TV and look at him. He was still peering through the camera lens, but his pants were open and his cock in his hand. He was jerking it up and down real hard. The head had turned a deep dark purple. Suddenly a drop of white sperm shot from its tip. Then a spurt. Then a jet. Then a stream. As Sam groaned in ecstasy, I joined him.

The camera caught every detail of my orgasm, although I wasn't aware of it at the time. I wasn't looking at the screen anymore. My eyes were riveted to Sam's pulsating prick, just as my fingers were fastened to my dripping sex slit. I shouted with pleasure, crying, "I'm coming. I'm coming."

I lay flat back on the bed with my legs spread wide as my fingers churned inside me. I could feel rivers of come flowing out of my pussy and onto my thighs. By the time my orgasm ended, the bedsheets were soaking wet. For a moment my eyes closed, shutting me into a magic world of sexual delight. Then I opened them again to look at Sam.

With a deep sigh, Sam turned off the camera. "You were fantastic," he said. "You've got the part."

"Play back the screen test," I begged in a breathless whisper. "I'm dying to see it."

We watched the tape together. It was much more stimulating for us than any of the rented pornos had ever been. We became aroused again almost instantly and ended up fucking before the tape was half over.

Since then, we've made lots of porno tapes, usually with the two of us performing. We really are good at it. Better than the professionals. We don't even bother renting movies anymore. We just play our own. I'm not really sure which is more fun—making them or watching them. We like to pretend that we've produced the films for a major studio and that they're available in video stores for other people to rent and see. Maybe some time we'll let you and Steve watch one of them.

12

You Two Do It While I Watch

According to many modern observers of the human condition, marriage in our society presents a dilemma—a problem for which all solutions are equally unsatisfactory. When morality requires one thing and nature another, they say, satisfaction is impossible. And, they add, morality and nature are at odds on the subject of monogamy.

When Moses presented the children of Israel with ten basic rules for a good and holy life, one of them prohibited adultery. Ever since then, Western society has expected marriage partners to be faithful to each other. Today, everyone acknowledges that this rule is frequently violated, although experts disagree about the reasons.

Swiss philosopher Denis de Rougemont offered one explanation in an influential work entitled *Love in the Western World*. Pointing to the myths that shape Western thought, he observed that the Western mind craves passion, drama, and romance. Since monogamous marriage cannot satisfy these needs, de Rougemont held that adultery is inevitable.

In *The Naked Ape*, zoologist Desmond Morris presented an evolutionary explanation, beginning with the claim that we are descended from a species of meat-eating primates. He said that when males started leaving the tribe every day to hunt, a system of sexual monogamy became necessary to prevent rivalries from tearing the society apart. He explained, however, that since hunting was a hazardous occupation, there was always the danger that a pair would be broken by the death of a partner. If pair-bonding was too exclusive, breeding inefficiency would result from such a death. So, he concluded, nature assured the survival of the species by seeing to it that each partner would continue to be sexually attracted to others.

Whatever the reason, there can be no doubt that many people find monogamy to be an unsatisfactory solution. In some parts of the United States, the divorce rate is nearly equal to the marriage rate. Many states have abandoned traditional beliefs in the permanence of marriage by making divorce available easily on a no-fault basis. The result is a system that some sociologists call serial polygamy, in which a person is likely to have several mates in a lifetime, although not simultaneously.

In 1973, writers Nena and George O'Neill suggested a different solution. In a book called *Open Marriage*, they argued that wherever monogamy has been the required standard of behavior, it has failed. They said that our society changes too fast and is too complex for one person to be able to satisfy all the sexual and nonsexual needs of any other person. They proposed restructuring our concept of marriage to permit each partner to engage in sexual intercourse with others. They admitted, however, that for many people such an arrangement would inevitably lead to jealousy.

Some of the couples to whom we talked have found a more practical solution. Recognizing that nature may cause them to be sexually attracted to persons other than their mates, they realize that acting on those attractions could be devastating to their marriage. So, to satisfy the conflicting requirements of nature and morality, they restrict their infidelities to the world of fantasy.

They imagine having sex with a television star, a political figure, or a passing acquaintance. They discuss these fantasies openly with their partners and even cast their partners in an observer's role so that they too can share the pleasures of the imaginary adventures. In this way they enjoy the benefits of sexual variety without taking any of the risks.

NANCY AND ALLAN

Iris:

Imagine my surprise when I learned that the health spa I had just joined was owned by Nancy, an old college acquaintance. When I knew Nancy at school, she had a reputation for promiscuity. According to rumor, she had slept with most of the men in our class, and even with some of the women. Although we weren't the closest of friends back then, Nancy had told me that many of the rumors were true and had described some of her sexual adventures to me in considerable detail. She seemed to feel the need to share her intimate secrets with somebody, and for some reason she picked me. Maybe it was because I so obviously enjoyed listening to her stories that she knew she would have my undivided attention.

In spite of the years that had passed since then, Nancy's body still looked like it did when we were in school, and I told her so. I had to admit that mine was more like a disaster zone. We laughed together for a while, and before long it was like old times again, with me listening in fascination as Nancy talked openly about her sex experiences. But now they involved her husband. . . .

* * *

When I bought this spa twelve years ago, the financial books were in a terrible state of disorder, so I hired an accounting firm to try to make some sense out of it. That's how I met my husband, Allan. He's the one they sent. As soon as he sat down and put on his glasses, I knew we'd end up getting married.

We had dinner together that night, and I took him home to bed with me. That's what clinched it. All the things that turned him on turned me on too. Since then, I haven't slept with anybody else. I haven't even felt the need. We both get all the variety we want by indulging our fantasies.

Right from the beginning, Allan liked me to tell him about affairs I'd had with other men while I was in college. I'd whisper, and he'd get so hot that sometimes I thought he was going to explode. Once, when I mentioned a brief relationship I had with a female roommate, he nearly wet himself. After he entered me, he made me describe my roommate's body and what I did with her in precise detail. I had never seen him so excited.

I treated him to that fantasy several times after that. Then one night, to keep the game fresh, I changed the description a little, using one of the women who works out here as my model. Allan realized what I was doing, and the idea especially turned him on. A few days later, when he came to the spa to work on the books, I saw him studying the women in the exercise class.

I noticed him watching one in particular and saw his cock getting stiff inside his pants as she moved around in her tight-fitting exercise clothes. He asked me her name, and I told him it was June. She was a model. Her body was already in great shape, but she worked out three times a week to make sure it stayed that way. She had great tits and the kind of ass that men can't help notice. Plus long blond hair that was a real attention-getter.

I could see that even though Allan was trying hard not to stare, his eyes were glued to the sight of her taut nipples outlined against her leotard. She had worked up a sweat, making the moist fabric cling to her like a second skin and leaving very little to the imagination. She never looked directly at Allan, but somehow, I got the feeling that she knew he was watching and she was kind of performing for him. Anyway, I don't mind who warms him up as long as I get to take him home.

That evening, Allan started undressing me the minute we got through the door of our house. When I was down to my panties, I fell to the floor, pulling him down on top of me. "I saw the way you were watching June," I said. "I've been watching her too."

I heard Allan moan softly.

"I've thought about putting my hands all over her body," I continued. "While you watch."

Allan sighed hungrily. "What would you do?" he asked.

"First, I'd feel her sweaty tits through the leotard," I whispered. "Then I'd pull it off, uncovering her completely."

"Yeah," Allan said. "Tell me more."

"I'd take her nipples in my mouth and suck them until they stand up like fat strawberries," I murmured. "Then I'd pull back my head so that you can get a good look while I just lick at them with the tip of my tongue. Would you like to see that?"

Before Allan had a chance to answer, I went on. "But mostly," I said, "I want to lick her pussy for you. I want to bury my face in it until my lips are covered with her juices. Then I want to kiss you on the mouth so that you can taste her pussy all over me."

Allan's delirious moans came right from his gut. He had his pants open and I could feel the tip of his prick pressing against the damp material that covered my crotch. In desperation, he pulled my panties to the side and inserted himself in me. "Go on," he begged. "What else are you doing with her?"

"I'm sliding my tongue deep into her crack, fucking her with it," I whispered. "When my tongue is coated with her passion fluid, I press it gently against her clit. It's thick and rigid. I'm running my tongue around it in little circles so that you can see it poking out from between her lips.''

I could feel Allan's cock throbbing inside of me as my description set his nuts on fire. It was getting to me too. The thought of making it with June while Allan watched had me as hot as it did him. Each time he thrust into me, my vaginal muscles tightened around him. My eyes were closed, and I was picturing June's naked body thrashing around under my oral caresses. I could practically feel her bush of soft blond hair tickling my lips. I could practically taste the sweet fragrance of her womanhood.

"I want to see her eating you, too," Allan groaned as he ground his body against mine.

"Yes," I said. "She's lying on her back with my face in her cunt. Slowly, without removing my tongue from her pleasure button, I move on my hands and knees until I'm straddling her head. My pussy is right over her mouth. I can feel her breath on it as I lower my crotch down against her. When she starts nibbling at my sex lips, I hunch back to open my slit wide around the tip of her nose. While her tongue penetrates me, my tongue bathes her clit and churns the froth surrounding it.''

"You're eating each other at the same time," Allan whispered in a voice made hoarse with lust. "And I'm watching the whole thing. You're driving me crazy, Nancy. Tell me how it feels."

At this point I was so carried away with my own description that I wasn't sure whether the ecstasy I was feeling was coming from Allan's cock driving inside me or from my imaginary sixty-nine with June.

"I'm sucking gently at her clit now," I murmured. "I'm showing her exactly what I want her to do to me. Soon she gets the point and starts sucking on my clit too. She knows you're watching us, and she wants to give you a good show.

"She's pulling my opening apart so you can see how big she's made my clit. My tongue is working as fast as hers. We're both going to come soon. I know your eyes are going back and forth from my tongue in her sex to her tongue on mine. I hear June moaning, and now the spicy fragrance of her has gotten even stronger. Her moans are getting deeper and deeper and faster and faster. I can taste the change in her pussy. Her clit is getting wetter and juicier. And now I can taste her orgasm as my mouth fills with her hot erotic juices. Oh, Allan, she's coming. She's coming in my mouth. And I'm going to come too. Inside her mouth, Allan. I feel her tongue against me, and I'm coming. Oh, God, I'm filling her mouth with my come."

Allan was pumping harder against me, driving his big cock right to the hilt in my pussy. I was coming with him at the same time that I was coming with June. The haze of fantasy swirled through my orgasm, so that I really felt her tongue and his cock all mixed up together. It was fantastic. Afterward, we just lay drifting together on the floor, tangled up in what was left of our clothes and feeling very well-satisfied.

Since then, our fantasy involves a different woman almost every time. Finding them is easy enough. The bodies come and go constantly in this place. Whenever Allan is in the mood for a special treat, he just comes in to work on the books and picks out my fantasy partner for the night. It's a way of filling our lives with sexual variety while remaining completely faithful to each other. I love every minute of it. I really get so into these fantasies that I actually live them. I get to have dozens of female lovers right under my husband's nose.

Who knows? Tonight it might be you. But don't look so worried. In my fantasy, you'll have the perfect body. I promise.

LUCILLE AND ROGER

Iris:

Our neighbors Lucille and Roger moved to the area where we live just a few months before we did. When our children were younger, school and community functions often brought us together, and we saw a lot of each other. No matter what was going on, however, we always knew that Lucille was not to be found outside her house in the middle of the day. During those hours, she prefers not to be disturbed. She calls it the best part of her day—her time for sitting in front of the TV and watching soap operas.

Sometimes, on mornings when Steve is teaching and Roger is at work, Lucille drops in to join me for a cup of coffee. Recently, she found me at the typewriter when she arrived. She started to apologize for the interruption, but as I poured the coffee, I assured her that I needed a break. Although she asked what

I was working on, I could tell from her tone that she was just being polite and really couldn't care less. When I told her about this book, however, her eyes lit up. I could see from her expression that I suddenly had all her attention.

"I'd like to read it some time," she said. "I'd like to know where other people get their fantasies from. I've always gotten mine from my soap operas . . ."

* * *

You know I've been addicted to soap operas for years. Maybe it's silly, but I actually feel that I know some of the characters personally. There's one actor in particular that I've even developed an imaginary relationship with. I've seen him play a few different roles in the soaps, but I've always thought of him as my personal Prince Charming.

It started some time ago. I'd be watching him on the screen, but my mind would be wandering. I'd imagine actually meeting him, maybe in a restaurant, where we'd sit and have a drink or eat dinner together. I had so many imaginary conversations with him that I suppose it was natural for my daydreams to go a little further.

I found myself wondering what it would be like to touch him. Before long, I started imagining it. I'd sit and stare at the TV, but in my mind I'd be fantasizing about making love with him. Oh, at first it was just romantic kind of stuff. I'd imagine that he was holding me in his arms and kissing me. But then it started to get sexier.

I began to fantasize about him stroking my breasts and kissing them. One day I discovered that, without realizing it, I had been touching them myself while watching him on the screen. At first, I felt kind of funny about it. But it felt so good that I just kept on doing it. After that, it got to be a regular event. I'd fantasize about my prince touching me, and I'd touch myself at the same time.

Eventually, we started having sexual intercourse—in my daydreams, of course. I would play with my breasts as I imagined the prince mounting me and taking me on the living room couch. It finally happened that I became so excited by my fantasies, I had to masturbate to relieve myself. Of course, I had masturbated before, when I was a teenager and even sometimes after Roger and I were married. But it had never felt so good before. I can't even describe it. There was just something in the combination of my daydreams about the soap-opera prince and the physical touching that made it special.

Anyway, after a while, I started looking forward to his show with the idea of fantasizing and masturbating while watching it. It was such a nice intermission in the middle of the day. And I really discovered lots of things about myself that way.

One day, I was stretched out on the couch with my skirt pulled up and my panties off, watching the TV and pleasuring myself. It felt so good and I was so into it that I didn't hear Roger drive up. For some reason, he came home from work early that day. I was deep into my fantasy and I felt a climax coming, so I closed my eyes tight and just let myself go. Afterward, I lay there for a few moments in a state of complete relaxation. Then I opened my eyes and saw Roger standing in the doorway with a big smile on his face.

"My God," I said. "How long have you been there?" I was so embarrassed. I had never done anything like that in front of Roger before. I felt guilty about it, as if he had caught me being unfaithful.

"Long enough," he said. "I really enjoyed that little show, Lucille. Maybe I should come home early more often."

My shame was turning to relief. Roger wasn't shocked or angry. He was excited. He came over to the couch and unbuckled his belt. Then he dropped his pants around his ankles and got on top of me without even taking off his clothes. It felt wonderful. Even though I had just finished masturbating, I had another orgasm almost immediately.

Later that night, Roger asked me to masturbate again while he watched. I tried, but I just couldn't do it. Finally, I explained that it was the fantasy about the soap-opera prince that got me started. I wasn't sure how Roger was going to react to this, but I just felt I had to tell him.

I was kind of surprised, because he seemed to like the idea. "Tell me about it," he said in a hoarse whisper. "Tell me about your fantasy."

At first, I was afraid that he'd be jealous if I told him everything, so I made it real vague. I said something like, "Oh, you know, I just sort of imagined what it would be like to get it on with this handsome actor."

But that didn't satisfy Roger. "No," he said. "Tell me the details."

I could tell by the way he was talking that it was a turn-on for him. And that got me excited, too. I knew that it would be safe to go on with the description. Little by little, I started to talk about my daydream, about the things I imagined being done to me.

I could see Roger getting hard as I spoke. And I was getting wet. So, while he was watching, I started touching myself again. Roger loved it. He was beside himself with excitement. For me, it was even better than the games I played alone in front of the TV.

After a while, Roger started stroking and kissing me. I kept whispering my fantasy about the prince, and Roger and I made love like we never did before. He was absolutely wild. He did things to me that he hadn't done in years. I had three orgasms in a row, something that had never happened to me before. By the time we ran out of energy, it was almost daylight.

My fantasy had turned into a true love story. Somehow, my secret relationship with Prince Charming had become something Roger and I could share. It added a thrill of variety for both of us, without giving him anything to be jealous about and without giving me any reason to feel guilty. Now I tell him about it all the time, masturbating while he watches me until we're both ready for hot sex play. It's become a regular part of our sex life.

I guess married people get lazy over the years, and they forget how important the foreplay can be. I think that was happening to Roger and me, and we never even realized it. But now that we've discovered this fantasy game, our sex life has gotten better than it ever was before. Even better than when we first got married.

ANDY AND MARY ELLEN

Steve:

Andy is an attorney I know. His wife, Mary Ellen, teaches at a state college while working toward her doctorate in political science. They are both in their mid-twenties. One evening recently, as Iris and I were having dinner in a San Diego restaurant, they stopped at our table to say hello. After introducing Andy and his wife to Iris, I invited them to join us for a drink.

Mary Ellen appeared a bit flustered by the invitation, but was about to sit down when Andy said, "Thank you very much, but we can't." Then, glancing mischievously at his wife, he added, "We have a date with the president."

Mary Ellen reddened at this and seemed to be trying to suppress a giggle.

I said, "Give him my best," and the young couple departed rather hurriedly.

A few weeks later when I happened to run into Andy at the county law library, I said, "Did you send the president my regards?"

The young attorney actually blushed. "It's just a little game we play," he mumbled. He was obviously embarrassed, but there was also a trace of pride in his manner as he added, "My wife and I have a fantastic sex life."

"Oh?" I said. I was interested in details, but didn't feel I knew Andy well enough to ask personal questions.

"I've never talked to anyone about this before,"

he said hesitantly. "But with all the sex research you've done, I have a feeling you'll understand . . ."

* * *

We're really into oral sex. I mean, we can do it for hours. My wife has this way of taking me right to the edge. Then, just when I feel that I can't hold off anymore, she squeezes my penis with her fingers and brings me down again. When I'm totally soft, she starts talking and brings it right up.

That's when we start playing this little game. It's kind of a fantasy that she weaves for me. She tells me we've been invited to the White House to have dinner with the president and his wife. It's an intimate little affair—just the four of us: Mary Ellen and me, the president and the first lady. Usually, it's a president from the past.

Anyway, after dinner, the four of us go into the oval office. The president's wife explains that they invited us to dinner because they're having a problem with sex. The problem is that she never learned how to give her husband head. She heard somewhere that Mary Ellen is great at it and was hoping that Mary Ellen would show her how.

At this point, Mary Ellen might say something like, "Is it all right with you if I demonstrate on the president?"

And I say, "You have to. It's your patriotic duty."

Now Mary Ellen begins stroking me gently. "First, I'd make him take off his pants and shorts," she'll say. "Then I'd rub him up and down like this while you and the first lady stand off to one side and watch."

As she strokes me, she talks about what she's doing, but she says she's doing it to him. Sometimes her descriptions are so vivid that I can close my eyes and actually see her holding the president's penis. "I squeeze it hard, like this," she says. Or "I tickle him under here, just like this."

Hearing her say it and feeling her do it at the same time really drives me wild. Sometimes she tells me that she can see the president's wife watching intently, trying to learn Mary Ellen's technique. Or she describes the way the first lady is becoming excited, with hard nipples jutting against the front of her dress and with beads of sweat breaking out on her upper lip. Mary Ellen has a great imagination.

After a while, she puts her mouth next to my penis and breathes on it. "I'm going to take him in my mouth now," she says. "I'm going to show his wife how it's done." She can keep it up for a long time, licking me and sucking me, and all the while pretending that she's doing it to the president. It drives me crazy.

Sometimes, when I feel like I can't hold out anymore, she changes the story to give me a turn. We've been invited to dine with the king and queen of a European country at the royal palace. The queen complains that her husband has been neglecting her. The king says that he doesn't have enough energy for sex and would appreciate it if I'd take care of his wife for him.

Mary Ellen tells me that the queen needs some good cunnilingus and that it would improve international relations if I helped out. At this point she takes my hand and puts it on her crotch. As I explore her with my fingers, she begins to describe the queen's clothing.

Usually, she has her majesty dressed in something expensive but royally drab, like a gray cashmere skirt and sweater. But she tells me that under the plain skirt the princess is wearing very sexy black lace lingerie. She describes how smooth and shapely the princess's legs are, in black stockings held up by a naughty black garter belt.

Holding my hand and rubbing it over her own body, she says that the queen is not wearing panties. She keeps up the talk all the while, describing the things I'm doing to her as if I was doing them to the queen. Like if I put a finger inside her, she'll say, "See how wet her highness is getting."

At this point she likes to give me specific instructions about what to do to the queen. "Why don't you kiss her down there?" she'll say, pushing my head toward her groin. "Why don't you lick her while the king watches."

I go nuts when she says something like, "Go ahead. Bury your face in her majesty's vagina. I don't mind. I love to watch you do it."

While I make love to her with my mouth, she continues to murmur and whisper about the things she sees me doing to the queen. Sometimes, she keeps it up until she has an orgasm. Other times, she makes me stop. Then, after a break, she goes back to her story about the president and the Oval Office.

13 Come Join the Orgy

One of the interesting things about language is the way it evolves, the way old expressions take on new meanings to satisfy the changing needs of society. An example of this can be seen in the treatment Webster's Third New International Dictionary gives to the phrase ''daisy chain.'' According to the main body of the dictionary, the traditional reference is to a string of daisies worn by selected students at certain graduation exercises. The Addenda Section, however, defines ''daisy chain'' as a group sexual activity in which each participant is in contact with two other persons.

The fact that this new usage has become common enough to require an entry in Webster's is a sign of the increased attention that group sex has been receiving in our society. The concept is not new, of course. It's not even uniquely human. Sea snails breed by forming circular daisy chains consisting of seven members, each penetrating the one in front while being penetrated by the one behind. Among humans, however, the idea is becoming more popular than ever before.

Pornographers seem to know this, since it is almost impossible to find an X-rated movie or book that doesn't contain at least one group or orgy scene. In a book entitled *Pleasures: Women Write Erotica,* psychologist Lonnie Barbach says that group sex is "possibly the single most popular sexual fantasy." Dr. Barbach suggests that one reason for this popularity is the increase in pleasure that comes from seeing and being seen, from hearing and being heard, while making love.

Recently, Herbert Margolis and Paul Rubenstein published a series of interviews with people who regularly participate in what the authors call "the groupsex phenomenon." In *The Groupsex Tapes,* interviewees offered many reasons for their participation. Some said that group sex enables them to monitor their spouses' extramarital activities and thus avoid insecurities. Others said that having sex in groups satisfies their need for variety while eliminating the possibility of dangerous emotional involvements. One participant said simply, "It's fun and not personal." Many explained that receiving sexual stimulation from more than one partner increases the available pleasure by increasing the available number of hands, mouths, and genitals.

Like Lonnie Barbach, we found group-sex fantasies to be extremely popular among the couples we interviewed. In truth, we collected enough of them to fill an entire book. In some, the presence of third or fourth persons was incidental to some other fantasy theme, like watching or being watched. A few of those are included in other chapters. In most, however, the idea of having a threesome, foursome, or more-some was central to the fantasy. We selected the ones in this chapter to give an idea of how diverse group sex fantasies can be.

One of the shared fantasies in this chapter—that of Tobi and Walter—was based on a real event. It is significant, however, that most of the couples who told us that they regularly share fantasies about group sex have never actually participated in such activities and have no real intention of ever doing so. While couples reporting other fantasies frequently say that they would like to actually try them out someday, those who enjoy imagining group sex usually recognize that reality is likely to be far less enjoyable.

LAWRENCE AND DOROTHY

Steve:

Iris and I have discovered that we can tell a great deal about people from the way they respond when we mention that we're writing a book. The extremely self-centered ones don't even ask what it's about. Those who are slightly less self-involved inquire politely, but don't really listen to the answer. Many others are genuinely interested until they hear that the book is about sexual fantasy. Then, prisoners of their own repressions, they quickly change the subject to avoid embarrassment.

Some people, however, seem to flash like a burst of lightning the moment they hear the word "sex." Their eyes are suddenly glued to our faces. Their ears are open and receptive, prepared to absorb every word. Their vibes tell us that we hold their interest in our hands. They broadcast excitement as they give us 100 percent of their attention.

When they learn that the book is about the erotic fantasies of sexually successful couples, they can't wait to tell us about their own sexual fantasies. They want to be part of the book. Perhaps they sincerely wish to make a contribution to the sexual happiness of others. Perhaps they just like the idea of anonymously exposing their own sexuality to the world.

Lawrence was one of the interested ones. He was an attorney whom I saw at the law library occasionally. We usually nodded to each other in vague greeting, but we never spoke until we found ourselves together one day in the library lounge.

Lawrence started a polite conversation: "Working on a case?"

When I told him that I was doing research for a book, he asked what it was about. When I answered, it was obvious that his interest stemmed from something more than mere conversational courtesy. "That's a great idea," he said. "Especially now, when fooling around can be your death. More couples ought to learn how to please each other with their imaginations. In fact, my wife and I have elevated sexual fantasy to a high art. It's kept us both faithful, and it's kept our marriage exciting and alive."

* * *

Dorothy and I have always been into sex. We were both virgins when we met, and neither of us has ever had anybody else. You might say that we learned everything we know from each other. And from pornography.

We love watching X-rated movies on the videocassette machine. When we first got married, we used to devote entire weekends to staying in bed and having sex while watching porno. We still do, sometimes. It's great to just lie there giving each other pleasure while the characters on the screen are doing the same.

In the beginning, it turned out to be a perfect way for us to get to know each other sexually. It was easy for me to tell what kinds of scenes turned Dorothy on the most, and it was easy for her to find out the same thing about me. In fact, that's how we both learned about oral sex. I never would have thought of going down on her if I hadn't seen her warm up whenever the actors did it on the screen. And I don't think she would have had the nerve for fellatio if she hadn't seen several porno queens survive it.

My biggest discovery was Dorothy's interest in the idea of a woman making it with two men. In one of the X-raters that we bought, there's a scene in which a big-breasted cutie takes on two studs at the same time. One of them is that guy with the elephant-sized penis. Dorothy used to play that scene over and over again, and I could always see her eyes getting glazed as she watched it.

At one point, the woman lies on top of the other guy, having intercourse with him while elephant-dick drives his giant erection into her anus. The camera comes in for a really amazing close-up of the woman's groin, with both openings stuffed. It really is quite a scene. Even I can imagine how good it must be for her to have two men at the same time. And, being a woman, it's only natural for Dorothy to get more involved in it than I do.

For some reason, though, she was embarrassed about it. She usually affected a casual attitude when selecting that particular movie and always found some excuse to replay the scene without having to admit that she especially liked it. Probably, she thought I'd be jealous if I knew that the idea appealed to her.

The fact is I always have been very possessive about Dorothy. I don't even like the idea of another man looking at her. I would go absolutely nuts at the thought of her having sex with someone else. But her fascination with big-dick and his partner didn't bother me at all. After all, they're just characters in a movie. I don't even think of them as real people. I could even get into the idea of seeing her with them. It turned me on almost as much as it did her.

One night, while that special scene was playing, I started some sex talk about it. First I said something about the size of that huge organ. Then, without waiting for Dorothy to say anything, I added, "Can you imagine how it must feel for her to have such a big one shoved inside?"

"Yes," Dorothy responded tentatively. "It is huge." She was actually blushing, and I knew that she was imagining it plunging into her own anus.

"Think about it," I said, stroking her backside. "Think about having it inside you. Think about him taking you from behind while I have you from in front."

Dorothy gasped. Reaching for me, she insistently

pulled me onto her. The second I got it in, she started to climax. I knew I had pushed the right button.

The following day, on my way home from the office, I stopped at one of those shops that sell sex books and marital aids. I was amazed at the collection of dildos that they had on display. They came in all different sizes and colors. A few had weird curves and ridges, but most looked like replicas of erect penises. I picked out a huge flesh-colored one, about the size of that guy's, and rushed home to surprise Dorothy with it.

As soon as I arrived, I ran into the bedroom and hid it under my pillow, waiting for exactly the right moment to give it life. After dinner, I suggested watching a porno movie, asking Dorothy to pick one out. I was pretty sure which one she would choose, and I was right. We got into bed nude and started to embrace as the movie built up to my wife's favorite scene. Then, just as the camera zoomed in on that massive organ, I pulled out the dildo and nuzzled it against Dorothy's sex.

She was startled. "My God," she said. "Where'd you get that?"

"This is Dick," I answered. "I thought you might like to meet him." As I spoke, I rubbed the tip of the rubber penis all over her mound. She immediately began writhing in passion, lying back and spreading her legs wide. I couldn't believe how fast she was getting aroused.

Slowly, I worked it into her, a little at a time, until it was buried deep inside. She sobbed and gasped with each stroke of the plunging dildo. I could see it stretching her outer membranes and I could imagine what was going on internally.

"How do you like Dick?" I asked softly. "Does it feel good to have him in you?"

"Oooh, yes," she moaned. "It feels wonderful." Then, closing her eyes to avoid looking into mine, she whispered, "I want to feel you inside me, too." She closed her legs to trap the dildo tightly in her vagina and rolled onto her side, pressing her bottom against my flesh-and-blood erection. With her hand, she spread her buttocks to invite me into her anus.

Seeing her so excited had whipped me up to a frenzy of arousal. I was breathless with desire. I hunched forward until my penis was poised at her back opening and then drove it in slowly but insistently. The intensity of her pleasure was contagious. We were like two wild creatures, expressing physical love as we had never done before.

I could feel the rubber penis filling her other opening. In my mind, I was sharing her with the big fellah, and I knew that in her mind, the dildo was attached to a living man. But it didn't bother me at all or make me jealous in any way, because in reality it was only she and I. We were rocking back and forth, meeting each other's desperate thrusts in a fantasy threesome that could never get in the way of our exclusive love. Our orgasms started almost at once and seemed to go on forever. It was a night we'll never forget.

Now we keep Dick in the drawer of Dorothy's night table so he can join us whenever we want him to.

DIANE AND CARL

Iris:

Recently, an acquaintance invited me to attend a woman's networking luncheon. She explained that each of the women at the luncheon would talk for a few minutes about whatever business she was in. The purpose was to give all of the people present an opportunity to advertise their services and to obtain business leads from one another. She suggested that the luncheon might be a good source of material for this book.

When it was my turn, I gave my little speech and invited the women to get in touch with me to talk about fantasies they shared with their mates. I noticed many interested faces in the group. A few days later, I heard from Diane, a computer specialist who had been at the luncheon. She offered to contribute a fantasy to the book so long as I promised to change her name.

I met her for lunch at a quiet and intimate restaurant. She was a little uncomfortable at first, but when I told her that Steve and I had interviewed numerous people about their fantasies, she seemed to relax and even to enjoy our conversation. She began by telling me that she and her husband, Carl, had been married for more than twenty years and that they had a satisfying sex life.

"We've done just about everything together," she said. "And those things we haven't done, we've imagined. We really like lying in bed and fantasizing together while we make love . . ."

* * *

The idea of having a threesome with another woman appeals to Carl, and the thought of it has a strange fascination for me too. Although we'd never actually do it, I've always known that it could be the basis of a hot fantasy. But the trouble was that I feel so possessive about Carl that even in fantasy I never could enjoy the idea of him having sex with anyone else. And thinking about myself with another woman was also a little scary to me. So, whenever Carl tried to get that one started, I resisted it and managed to change it around to just the two of us.

Then Heather came along. Heather is Carl's new boss. She is a beautiful young woman who makes no bones about the fact that she's gay. After I learned this about her, I found myself trying to picture her making love with another woman. The scenes I imagined were so exciting that sometimes I even put myself in them, in spite of my sense of shame at thinking about it.

One night in bed, Carl was stroking my breasts when he tried a threesome fantasy again. "I've always imagined you touching another woman's tits just like this," he whispered.

I could tell by his tentative tone that he fully expected me to turn it around as usual. But I surprised him. "Yes," I murmured. "I can see myself stroking Heather."

I was as surprised as he was. I didn't plan to say it; it just slipped out. Then I realized that Heather would be a perfect fantasy partner for us. She was beautiful, but she was safe. Since she didn't care for men, I didn't have to worry about her and Carl. I could imagine her joining us in bed without suffering any pangs of jealousy.

Carl loved the idea. "Heather?" he gasped. Then he smiled in understanding. "Of course. Heather," he repeated. "What are you and Heather doing?"

"I'm holding Heather's nipples," I said, my eyes tightly closed. "They're all erect and hard. I'm rolling them in my fingers like this." I demonstrated on myself, feeling Carl's excitement rise. "Now I'm lifting her breasts with my hands and squeezing them. Just like this." I massaged my own mounds as I spoke.

"And what's Heather doing?" Carl asked breathlessly.

"She's licking me and sucking my nipples," I said, looking up at Carl. His eyes were glazed with arousal. I pulled his head against my breast and thrust one of my nipples into his mouth. He caught it gently between his teeth and ran the tip of his tongue over it, moaning softly.

"Yes," I whispered. "She's sucking me like that. Exactly like that. She's licking one of my tits while you lick the other."

I knew it excited him to hear that, and it excited me even more. I could imagine two mouths nuzzling and nibbling at me simultaneously. The idea that one of them was a woman's made it especially erotic.

"Is she making you feel good?" Carl asked.

"Yes," I sighed. "Heather's wonderful at it. She's an expert at pleasing another woman. She knows just what to do." In my mind I almost felt Heather's lips on my turgid flesh. Her tongue was softer than Carl's. Her touch was lighter and gentler. She was completely alert to my responses and eager to satisfy all my desires. I wanted to do things to her too.

"I'm stroking her pussy now," I whispered. "I feel her bushy hair bristling with excitement. Her lips are dripping with liquid. Slowly, I slip my finger into her."

I imagined rubbing my hand over another woman's moist sex as my husband watched. I described the way it felt to wallow in the wetness of her heated opening. "She's so nice and warm inside, Carl. I can feel the sweet sensuous folds of flesh," I murmured. "I'm swirling my finger around in her thick woman juices." I thrust a finger inside my own vagina, imagining that it was Heather's.

Carl held me in his arms and pressed his erect penis against my thigh as I spoke. I could feel him throbbing with desire. My words and images were exciting us both.

"She's going down on me," I said, picturing her lips nibbling at my vulva. "She's sucking my clit."

"Does her mouth feel like mine?" Carl asked in a croaking whisper.

"No," I said. "It's different. It's a woman's mouth. She's doing things that only a woman can know about." I took his penis in my hand and stroked it softly. "I want to feel both of you at the same time," I said, my voice trembling. "I want to feel your cock in me while her tongue licks my button."

Carl's penis jumped. "Yes," he groaned. "I want to fuck you on the inside while she eats you from the outside. And I want to see you touch her too."

I pictured it at once. "She's lying on her back,"

I said. "She's all naked and she's spread out for both of us to see. Her tits are pointing straight up in the air and her legs are apart so her pussy is completely exposed." As I spoke, I got onto my hands and knees.

"I'm straddling her now," I continued. "My pussy is just a fraction of an inch away from her mouth. I can feel her hot breath against me. It's making my clit swell. Can you see it?"

Carl was behind me, looking at my pussy. Incredibly, the fantasy was starting to feel like reality. I could actually see Heather's wet vagina puckering up at me as I waved my backside at Carl in a sexy circle. I lowered my head and inhaled deeply. I could actually smell the fragrance of Heather's sex.

"Oh, Carl" I said. "Put it in me. Put your cock in me while Heather licks me from underneath." I could already feel the tip of Carl's massive penis nudging at the back-turned opening of my vagina. I was so wet that Carl was able to drive it in to the hilt in a single hunching stroke. "Oooh, Carl, that feels just wonderful," I cried. "And I feel Heather's tongue, too. Probing me. Searching for my clit. Yes, yes, she's found it now. Oh, God, Carl, I can't believe it. I'm having both of you at the same time. Oh, nothing ever felt this good before. Oh, she's licking my clit while you're fucking me."

I was so worked up that I forgot that it was a fantasy. I was experiencing the most perfect oral sex and the best possible intercourse all at the same time. The combination of Carl's penis and Heather's tongue was bringing me to new heights of pleasure.

No one sex partner could have given me all the sensations I was getting from Carl and Heather together.

I pictured Heather's pubic mound bumping up and down in front of my face as she tongued me. "I'm going to lick Heather's pussy now, Carl," I blurted. "Close your eyes and watch me. Watch my tongue go into her. Oh, she tastes so good. I want us all three to come together."

"Oh, Diane," Carl wailed. "You're driving me wild. Oh, yes, I'm going to come in you while Heather sucks your clit." His words vibrated through my body. I could feel his hairy scrotum bumping against me as he drove harder and harder. At the same time, I could feel Heather's soft feminine tongue teasing and tantalizing my most sensitive spot.

Carl shouted as I had never heard him shout before. "I'm coming. Oh, Diane, I'm coming." I felt him spurting inside me as his orgasm began. I imagined his semen filling me to overflowing and then dripping out to wet the woman's mouth that licked and lapped at me. The sensation carried me over the brink.

"Oh, yes," I moaned. "I'm coming too." My mind whirled with surges of ecstasy that emanated from my womb and inflamed my entire body. Images of Carl's penis and my vagina, and my clitoris and Heather's mouth, and Heather's vulva and my tongue, washed over me like a flood, lifting and tossing me in a rushing torrent of sexual passion. I cried and sobbed and wailed until all the glorious blasts of emotion were spent. Then I eased forward to lie facedown on the bed with Carl's softening penis still clutched hotly inside me.

We lay like that for a long time, basking in the torrid afterglow. Later, we agreed that it was the best sex we ever had and promised each other that we would do it again that way real soon. We did, of course, and we've done it like that many times since then. Not every time; I don't think either of us could stand that. Just once in a while, when we're both in the mood for a special sexual treat.

It works out perfectly for Carl. It gives him the chance to be in bed with two women at the same time without making me feel threatened or jealous. And I've discovered that I love the idea of having sex with another woman. If I had that kind of fantasy all alone, I'd probably worry about whether I was turning gay. But somehow the fact that Carl is there and that I'm kind of doing it for him instead of just for myself makes it okay.

TOBI AND WALTER

Iris:

When Steve and I celebrated our twenty-fifth wedding anniversary, our children surprised us by sending us on a Mississippi riverboat cruise with wonderful Cajun-style foods and nonstop Dixieland music. In the boat's dining room we were assigned to share a table with Tobi and Walter. They were both physicians, and as soon as they learned that

Steve was a lawyer, they started complaining about the high cost of malpractice insurance. Steve told them bluntly that he found it hard to sympathize with people who make enough to pay more for their insurance alone than a law professor earns in a year.

For a while, I began to fear that our cruise would be a disaster because we had to sit with these people in the dining room three times a day. But when we mentioned that we were writing a book about couples' sexual fantasies, we discovered that we had a common ground, and our conversation improved notably. It turned out that Tobi and Walter were just as interested in talking about sex as we were, and we actually found ourselves looking forward to joining them for meals.

One day while Steve and Walter were answering trivia questions in the game room, Tobi and I went to the Paddlewheel Lounge for a drink. As we sipped our juleps, Tobi offered a fantasy for our book. She said that she had discussed it with Walter and he approved of her telling me about it as long as he wasn't present at the time. . . .

* * *

When I was in medical school, I used to go to some really wild parties. Everybody would get drunk or stoned and there would be lots of loose sex. I think it might have had something to do with the fact that after putting in all those grueling hours, we all wanted to let our hair down. And because we spent all our time studying about the human body, we tended to be rather casual about our own.

I met Walter at one of those wild parties. The alcohol was flowing like a waterfall and there were enough drugs to open a pharmacy. I had never been so inebriated before in my life. I was so high that I was lying naked on the floor, having sex with several men at the same time. Every now and then, one of them would drop out and watch for a while as another took his place. Through the haze of my intoxication, I was aware of penises slipping in and out of my vagina, my mouth, and both my hands. I felt fingers on my nipples, squeezing them and making them tingle. I felt hands stroking my buttocks and clitoris until I was beside myself with pleasure.

I realized that I was making quite a display, but that was exciting me even more. Whenever I opened my eyes to look around, I would see the faces of men and women staring down at me. Sometimes, I wasn't sure whether the hands and tongues that were on me were male or female. And I didn't even care. All I knew was that I felt good all over.

In the middle of all this, I saw Walter come into the room. I recognized him vaguely as a fellow student who was a year or two ahead of me, but I had never spoken with him before. I closed my eyes again and abandoned myself to the erotic sensations without thinking any more about him. But it seemed that whenever I opened my eyes, he was standing over me, watching the action. There was something that made him attractive to me even as intoxicated as I was. I remember feeling kind of disappointed that he was doing nothing but watching. Finally, when I saw him unbuckle his belt and get ready to join the orgy, my excitement increased.

I lost track of him as hands and penises and tongues engaged my emotions and carried me back into my erotic trance. Someone had rolled me onto my side and was licking my anus. Two different mouths were sucking at my breasts. A penis was nudging at my lips, filling my mouth with that sexy salty taste. Suddenly, I felt my vagina being stretched open as it had never been stretched before. I was sure that there were two penises penetrating it at the same time, stuffing me with their hard, throbbing flesh. Sobbing in ecstasy, I opened my eyes to see what two men were having intercourse with me simultaneously.

For a moment, I couldn't focus. Everything was a blur of naked skin and pulsating sex organs. Then, to my shock, I realized that there was only one penis inside of me—a penis so huge that it felt like two. All of the other sensations faded into the background. The fingers that explored me so freely, the scrotums that I felt in my hands, the mouths that were nibbling at my nakedness, were like nothing compared to this giant, driving erection.

I blinked my eyes to clear the mist and realized that Walter was between my thighs, buried deep inside me. Every movement of his body increased my pleasure. It was Walter, and Walter alone, who was taking me to the peak of passion. I wanted desperately to kiss him, but there were too many other people in the way. I passed out in the middle of the most furious climax of my life.

The following morning, I woke up in a clean bed, alone and sick as a dog. I had no idea of where I was or how I got there, and I was too weak to worry about it. My head spinning, I groaned in discomfort.

Immediately, a hand stroked my forehead and a masculine voice said, "How are you feeling?"

I looked up and saw Walter. Suddenly, as the events of last night flashed through my mind, I found myself feeling horribly ashamed and wishing that I was dead. Closing my eyes, I turned to bury my face in the pillow. I started crying, unable to deal with my embarrassment.

"Oh, God," I said. "You must think I do that sort of thing all the time. I don't know how I'm going to show my face in class again with all those people."

"Don't worry," he said gently. "Everybody gets drunk some time. Most of the others won't even remember what happened." He told me that after I passed out, he was worried about me, and that he had carried me to his apartment, which happened to be in the same building as the party.

When I started to sit up in bed, he handed me a robe, saying that he didn't know what had become of my clothes. He mixed me some kind of breakfast drink that he said was guaranteed to cure hangovers. After a while, he took me home.

I appreciated his kindness, but I was still too sick to think much about him. Later, though, I realized that I wanted to know him better. In the weeks that followed, I tried approaching him at the school. He was polite, but he seemed rather distant. One of my friends who knew him told me that Walter thought me a little too promiscuous for him.

I was so attracted to him that I refused to give up. Eventually my persistence paid off: we began dating. Two years later, we were married. For a long time,

Walter made it clear that he did not want to discuss our first meeting. It bothered him to think about all the men who had me before he did, and so publicly. At first, he wouldn't even let me bring it up.

I wanted to discuss it, though, because I realized that this would always be a problem with us otherwise. Also, I must admit that I found the memory of that crazy night very exciting and I didn't want to have to keep that excitement all to myself. I wanted him to share the pleasure and to realize that none of those other people meant anything at all to me. Besides, it wasn't healthy for him to feel all that resentment and just keep it inside. I knew that I had to find some way to turn that negative into a positive.

I waited until the time was exactly right. Then one night, while we were making passionate love, I subtly brought up the taboo subject. "Walter," I whispered, "You're the most fantastic lover in the world." I could feel his ego expanding along with his penis. "You're the only man who stands out as an individual in my recollections of that crazy orgy when we met."

Walter was a little uncertain of how he should be feeling at this point, so I went on. "There were hands all over me," I said, "and several men had climbed on and off me. But it wasn't until I felt you inside me that I reached a climax." He was silent. "Everything changed the moment you entered the room," I continued. "And when you penetrated me, I thought I was feeling two men at once. You were so big and so hard. You were the best."

For the first time, Walter had allowed me to talk about it without objection. But, still, he had said nothing himself. A few nights later, I brought it up again while we were having sex. I began by talking about what a good lover he was. Little by little, I described some of the other sensations I had felt, repeating, every now and then, that none of it compared to what I felt with him. He listened in silence for a while, and then said, "It couldn't have been too terrible, though."

I sensed that he was beginning to accept the idea, that in his own way he was even encouraging me to talk about it. I guess he was feeling more secure about me and about our relationship. It must have been obvious to him that I found the memories arousing, and he was beginning to want to share in my excitement. Keeping it simple, I described some of the acts I had performed that night. As I did, I felt my passion increasing, and his along with it. We came together as I spoke.

As time went on, we both became less inhibited about the subject. Finally, we reached a point where he would ask me for specific descriptions, like how it felt to have one penis in my vagina and another in my mouth at the same time. Over the years, we've enhanced our sex life with our fantasy talk. Sometimes, when I run out of memories, I make up details. At this point, I'm not really sure anymore what parts of it actually happened and what parts are pure fantasy. All I really know is that fantasizing together about that orgy has turned out to be the best of all possible aphrodisiacs and has kept our sex life happy and healthy.

In my opinion, a book like yours can help a lot of

couples benefit from their sexual fantasies. I say this not only as a doctor but as a sexually contented woman. That's why Walter agreed to let me tell you this.

14   We Tried Acting It Out

To most of the couples with whom we spoke, doing the things they fantasized about would be unthinkable. After all, the best thing about fantasy is that it allows people to experience pleasures in the imagination that they could not ordinarily experience in reality. For this reason, couples tend to fantasize about things they consider impossible.

The more familiar an idea becomes, however, the less outlandish it begins to seem. Even imaginary experiences can have this effect. After seeing movies like *E.T.* and *Cocoon,* for example, visits from interplanetary travelers don't seem as impossible as before. Similarly, after repeatedly sharing imaginary sexual experiences, some couples find that the barriers that stop them from living those experiences no longer appear insurmountable. Their next stop is to try doing what previously they only imagined.

Although these couples are a minority, their experiences usually turn out to be quite dramatic. Attempts to live out shared erotic fantasies seem to fall into two distinct categories. Some discover that reality is even sweeter than fantasy, that imagined pleasures are more intense when actually experienced. Others find bitterness in efforts to actualize their shared dreams.

All the people in this chapter enjoyed sharing erotic fantasies with their spouses. When they attempted to act out their shared fantasies, however, their responses varied considerably. For two of the three couples involved, acting it out was even better than fantasizing about it. A perfect combination of circumstances made it possible for their wildest sexual dreams to come true. The joyful reality they experienced will go on to provide the substance for future fantasies, which may, in turn, be actualized at some subsequent time. For the other couple, however, the result was disastrous.

MATT AND PENNY

Steve:

Several years ago a prominent men's magazine hired me to write a series of articles about sex and the law. One of the articles was to be about massage parlors and the way courts in various states view them. While researching the subject at the county law library, I got into a conversation with a group of lawyers I met there. After describing what I was working on, I asked whether any of them ever had experience with massage parlors.

Matt, a seasoned attorney in his mid-fifties, smiled. "I did," he said. "Just once. It was a present from my wife."

All the men expressed curiosity, urging Matt to tell the story. After a little coaxing, he obliged . . .

* * *

My wife, Penny, and I have been married for more than twenty years, and in that time neither of us has been unfaithful. Sometimes I wonder how it can be that we've never gotten stale for each other. I think it's because we've always been willing to experiment with our sexuality.

One of our favorite activities is giving each other massages. We put a foam-rubber mattress on the dining-room table and take turns being massaged and massaging. I like to stroke her body for a long time, touching places that get her aroused and then moving on to less erogenous areas before things get out of hand. I can tell she likes it too.

Sometimes when it's my turn to receive, we pretend that Penny is a girl working in a massage parlor and that I'm just a customer. At first, she keeps the massage nonsexual, rubbing my back and my legs and my chest. She's no professional, of course, but she's pretty good at it. Usually I get a hard-on before she's half-done, but she just ignores it and keeps on rubbing me. Then, when I feel like I can't stand it any longer, she starts stroking my cock. I'm supposed to remain completely passive, to keep my hands off her and just let her do everything.

A few months ago, on my birthday, Penny announced that she was taking me out to dinner at the best restaurant in town. She said that she had made reservations for eight-thirty, but first she had a birthday surprise for me. I asked what it was, but she said, "If I told you, it wouldn't be a surprise."

When we got into the car, she drove out to the suburbs. It took almost an hour, and we ended up in a neighborhood with which I wasn't familiar. Penny seemed to know just where she was going, however, and we soon found ourselves on a quiet residential street. She parked the car in front of a private house and said, "Here we are. Let's go inside."

As we walked toward the front door, she said, "This is Crystal's house. She's a professional masseuse. I've arranged for you to have the best massage of your life. And I'm going to watch so that maybe I can learn a few tricks of the trade." She rang the doorbell and lowered her voice to add, "And after the massage there's a special birthday treat."

A moment later the door was answered by an attractive young woman in shorts and a brief halter top. "Come in," she said. "You must be the birthday boy."

She led us through the house to a room that served as her work studio. It was painted white and was as clean as a hospital. In the middle of the room was a massive, padded, wooden massage table covered with a crisp white sheet. Gesturing toward it, she said, "Take off your clothes and lie facedown on the table. I'll be right back."

I looked quickly at Penny and then back at the girl. "All my clothes?" I asked.

"Everything," Crystal said as she left the room.

Penny smiled and nodded. "How can you have a massage with your clothes on?" she said. "Relax, honey. You're going to enjoy this."

I must admit I felt a little awkward undressing in front of my wife when we both knew that the young woman would be coming right back into the room. But I did as I had been instructed and lay facedown on the table, carefully covering my ass with a towel. I watched Penny seat herself comfortably in an armchair. A moment later, the young masseuse returned.

She stood by the side of the table for a moment and then whipped the towel off me. I could feel my face reddening. I watched Crystal pour oil from a bottle onto her hands. Then she began anointing my back and shoulders with structured and educated movements.

From the first stroke, I knew this was going to be something. It always feels good to be touched, of course, but there's a real difference when it's done by an expert. Crystal rubbed and kneaded my back and legs for at least twenty minutes, covering every square centimeter with warmed and sensuous oil.

Every once in a while, her fingertips stole between my thighs and grazed the back of my scrotum or strayed erotically over the crack of my ass. Whenever it happened, I wondered whether it was accidental or whether she had done it on purpose. I looked at Penny to see her reaction, but she didn't even let on that she had noticed. She just sat there watching intently as the attractive young woman expertly touched me all over. I found myself getting very excited and had to wiggle a little to keep my hard-on from pressing uncomfortably into the padded tabletop. I was kind of embarrassed about it and hoped that Penny wouldn't discover my condition.

Before I could give it any more thought, though, I felt Crystal's hands working gently but firmly to turn me onto my back. I tried to resist, but I couldn't without making a scene. So I complied, even though my erection was standing straight up like a flagpole. For a few seconds, I avoided looking at Penny. But then I heard her giggle, and my heart told me everything was all right. When I glanced at her face, she smiled and blew me a kiss.

The girl just ignored my erection and continued giving me a terrific and very professional massage. I could feel her manipulating every muscle individually as her fingers pressed and kneaded my arms, shoulders, and chest. When she worked her way down toward my loins, my swollen dick started to throb.

Her trained fingers massaged their way toward my thighs, her knuckles brushing lightly over my penis and scrotum as they went by. I inhaled sharply, forgetting for a moment that my wife was sitting right there. Then I looked toward Penny and saw her smile again. I still wasn't sure whether the sex contact was deliberate or accidental. All I knew was that my cock was as hard as a rock, and was pulsating to some inner rhythm.

Crystal's strong fingers kneaded the flesh of my inner thighs, working their way down toward my knees and then up again toward my groin. It seemed that each pass brought her closer to my sex organs. I wanted to moan with delight, but my wife was sitting right there. I didn't know how to react, so I just lapped it up in silence.

After fifteen minutes or so of this exquisite torture, Crystal's hands slid up my legs directly to my crotch. Suddenly, she was holding my testicles in one hand and my penis in the other. This was obviously no accident.

Startled I started to sit up. "Er, ah, hold it," I said. "I mean, don't hold it. I mean, stop. Er, I mean, maybe this isn't—"

Penny was at my side immediately, putting her hand on my chest and pushing me gently down again. "It's all right, Matt," she said. "This is the special birthday treat I mentioned earlier. Just relax and enjoy it. I'm having a wonderful time. I don't mind it a bit." She returned to the armchair and sat down again.

With her assurance, I lost all feeling of hesitation. I lay back comfortably and gave myself over to the fabulous sensations. Crystal really knew her stuff. She stroked me for a long time, bringing me right to the edge of climax and then backing away just before I could start to come. I kept looking at Penny to make sure it really was all right. She was breathing heavily and looked like she was having almost as good a time as I was.

That was the best part of it. I mean, the girl had a real nice touch, but the most exciting thing was that my wife was sitting there watching it all. Not only did she not object to it, but she was really enjoying it too. It was better than fantasy. We were actually doing it. Together.

At last, when I didn't think I'd be able to hold out any more, Crystal brought me off. It was really something the way she seemed to be touching all the sexual parts of me at once. One hand was sliding sensuously up and down over the shaft of my penis while her fingers tickled the head and her other hand played over my scrotum.

"I'm going to come," I said tentatively, looking at my wife again, still feeling that I needed her permission.

"Yes," Penny whispered hoarsely. "I want to see you come."

She just sat there watching while my climax overtook me. I guess I closed my eyes while it was happening. When I opened them again, Penny was standing over me, smiling. While Crystal cleansed me with a hot towel, Penny kissed me on the lips. "Happy birthday," she said.

Later, over dinner in the restaurant, Penny and I talked about it. She told me how exciting it had been for her to watch as the young woman stroked and pleasured me. I told her how good it felt and how thrilling it was to know that she had arranged it all and that she had watched it happen. We got so turned on talking about it that we rushed home right after dinner to make love like a couple of passionate youngsters.

Since then, we've talked about it a lot. It still hasn't lost its wonderfully arousing effect on both of us. And, you know, I can't wait for Penny's birthday.

SCOTT AND LINDA

Iris:

When Steve and I first arrived in the San Diego area, we were writing adult fiction for a local book publisher. Seeking a quiet place to live and work, we rented a rustic cabin about forty-five miles from the city in what San Diegans call the back country. Our cabin was one of two located on a thirty-acre ranch. The other was rented by Linda and Scott, a recently married couple from the Midwest. Scott was in the navy, assigned to a ship based in San Diego.

Since we were usually busy writing, we did not see very much of Linda and Scott except for an occasional social call. They were fascinated to learn that we were authors of erotic fiction and always asked about our work during their infrequent visits. They held us in a kind of awe, apparently believing that, since we wrote about sex, we knew everything there was to know about it.

One afternoon when I was home alone, Scott dropped in for a chat. He talked about the weather for a few minutes, but his mind was obviously elsewhere. Finally, in a rush of words, he said, "I'd like to tell you something. I need to talk about it and I can't think of anyone else I could tell it to." He lowered his voice. "It's about Linda and me. And sex . . ."

* * *

Linda and I weren't married very long when I was transferred here. We rented this cabin because San Diego was just too big for us. We felt more at home living in the country. We grew up in a small town and we went steady in high school. I was her first boyfriend and she was my first girlfriend. In our town, high-school kids weren't supposed to know much about sex. Even a good-night kiss was considered improper before at least three dates. We were real naive when we first got married.

For the first few months of our marriage, we were awkward and clumsy. We were discovering things that kids who grow up in big cities probably learn a whole lot earlier. Anyway, after a while, we became more comfortable with each other and we started experimenting with different positions and ideas. We played all kinds of games. Like once, when I took nude pictures of her with an instant camera.

I really liked carrying those pictures around with me. I even showed them to some of my buddies on the ship. Most of the guys I hung out with at the time weren't married yet, and I was kind of a big man because I was. Everybody used to joke about how much sex I must be getting, and I liked it. Showing them those pictures was a way of bragging, I guess. Now I realize what a childish game it was.

Anyway, at the time, I liked it when the guys would talk about how sexy they thought Linda was. I considered myself lucky and figured that their cracks about my wife were personal compliments to me for having a woman who was hot enough to pose nude. I didn't mind it when they talked about how much they'd like to get their hands on her. I guess I kind of encouraged them.

My closest buddy at the time was a guy named Moose. And he really deserved the name. He was built like King Kong and had the strength of a gorilla. There wasn't a guy on the ship who didn't respect Moose's build. I envied him, probably because I've always been slight and underweight.

Moose really got off on the pictures I showed him

of my naked wife. He used to ask to see them all the time, and his eyes bulged whenever he examined them. Moose was the kind of guy that felt at liberty to say whatever came to his mind. Once, while looking at the snapshots, he licked his lips and said, "Boy, would I like to fuck her."

That night I told Linda what he said, and I could see that it really turned her on. She put my hand on her to show me how wet she was. It was a real thrill for me to know that I was getting her so hot by the way I was talking. The fact that she was thinking about Moose didn't bother me at all, because it was my words that were turning her on.

I really played up Moose's size, putting three fingers into her and telling her to think of it as Moose's dick. She came so fast that it was over almost before it began. Afterward, she gave me a really great fucking. I felt I had discovered a wonderful new way of having sex.

After that, we played that same game lots of times. When we got into bed, I would talk to her about Moose while I stroked and played with her. It always got her hot, and that always made me even hotter. Usually, her orgasms were so good that she went out of her way to do real good things for me too. I enjoyed this fantasy game more than I had ever enjoyed any game in my life. But I should have left it that way.

One day when I was having trouble with my car, Moose offered to drive me home from the ship. We stopped to buy a couple of bottles and drank a little in Moose's car on the way home. By the time we got there, we were already feeling pretty high, but we kept right on drinking. I should have known better than to get as drunk as I did, and I shouldn't have let Linda drink quite so much either. Before we knew it, we were all rip-roaring plastered.

Moose was flirting with Linda, and once I even thought I saw him pat her ass. Linda didn't say anything, so I wasn't really sure I had actually seen it. Somehow, not being sure was kind of exciting. I remembered the fantasies Linda and I had talked about, and in my alcoholic haze, I was starting to get them mixed up with reality.

When Moose left the room, Linda sat in my lap and started grinding against me. I was getting really horny, but more than that, I wanted to show Moose what a big man I was. I wanted to show him that my sexy wife would do anything I said.

So when Moose came back in, I called him over and told Linda to go ahead and check him out. He came and stood in front of her. I guess I didn't realize that Linda was really going to do anything. To my surprise, though, she started rubbing him through his pants. Then, before I knew it, she opened them up and took out his dick.

Moose's dick is about twice the size of mine, and I started to get uncomfortable almost immediately. When Linda took it in her hand and began stroking it, I felt just awful. I got cold all over and started to get sick to my stomach. I wanted to tell her to stop, but I was ashamed. After all, I had started the whole fucking thing.

I thought that things couldn't get any worse, but then he started undressing her. Within seconds, he had her tits out and he was touching and pulling on them. It was one thing for me to show him naked pictures of her, and another for her to be undressed right in front of him. As his fingers played with her nipples, I wanted to die right on the spot. I stood up to put a stop to it, but just couldn't. I had this strange idea that it would make me look like some kind of wimp if I admitted the way I was feeling. And I was getting so sick that I just had to leave the room.

I ran to the bathroom and threw my guts up, not really because of what I had been drinking, but because of what I had been seeing. I stood there for a minute, heaving and choking, and then I decided to go back inside and stop them. But when I returned to the living room, it was too late.

There they were. Moose was standing up holding Linda's ass. She had her legs wrapped around his hips, and he had his cock buried deep inside of her. The sight of it made me want to scream, but I just stood frozen in the doorway, paralyzed with horror and still unable to say that I wanted it to stop at once. I remember thinking that it would be all right as long as neither of them came. But in seconds they were both shouting and moaning and announcing that they were coming together.

I started to get sick again as I imagined jets of Moose's sperm shooting into her pussy. Linda was carrying on so much that I knew that she was having a better orgasm than I had ever been able to give her. Moose was so much bigger than me, and so much stronger. I had never fucked Linda in that position. I didn't really have the physical strength for it. And Moose's cock was so much longer than mine that I'm sure I had never been in her so deep.

When those thoughts hit me, I knew that somehow it would never be the same for me and Linda. I couldn't stand being in the room a minute longer. I had to get out. I couldn't bear to see any more. I went back into the bathroom and stayed there as long as I possibly could. When I finally came out, Moose left right away and I was alone with Linda. I never felt so insecure in my life. I couldn't look at her. I couldn't even talk to her.

When we went to bed, Linda still didn't know how I felt. She obviously had enjoyed herself tremendously and she wanted to tell me all about it. But every word she spoke made things worse. Finally I told her to shut up and I rolled over, pretending to go to sleep. But I couldn't sleep. I just lay there for hours, crying.

I realize now that getting Linda to act out that fantasy was the worst mistake I ever made in my life. We've talked about it, and Linda understands how I feel. But deep down, I know that she really liked it and she wishes it could happen again some time. I really don't know if I'll ever get over it.

KELLY AND ERIC

Iris:

Kelly has been our travel agent for the past ten years. During that time, she helped plan the transportation for many of Steve's lecture tours and for a few of our vacations. Like most people in her business, Kelly loves to take trips. She and I have had many pleasant conversations about our travel experiences.

Recently, when I went to see her about some plane tickets, I mentioned that Steve and I were working on this book. Her smile showed the kind of interest that led me to ask whether she and her husband, Eric, might have a fantasy to contribute. For a moment, she looked embarrassed. Then she grinned.

"I've never told anybody this," she said. "And you're probably going to put it in your book. But it's such a great story, that I've got to tell it to you . . ."

* * *

Eric and I have always had a very satisfying sex life. Sometimes we spend entire weekends just lying in bed and making love. We call them marathons. When we're planning to have one, we usually rent five or six porno movies to watch on the video and keep us hot.

The kinds we like best have threesome scenes, especially where a man and woman both work on another woman. We go out of our way to find those, because they never fail to turn us both on. Then we lie in bed watching those scenes and playing with each other. While Eric strokes and pets me all over, we imagine that there's another woman with us and that she's also petting and stroking me. Sometimes we pretend that it's one of the women in the movie we're watching.

That gets me really excited, because I've always wondered what it would be like to have another woman make love to me. And with Eric doing things to me at the same time, it would be even better. It makes a great fantasy for us. Sometimes Eric takes the lead, telling me all the things that are going on, and sometimes I do. It always makes us both really hot. Sometimes, while we're doing it, I have three or four orgasms in a row. Eric absolutely loves when that happens.

I don't think either of us ever seriously considered the possibility of doing anything like that. In the first place, we wouldn't have known how to find someone to do it with. It certainly couldn't be anybody we know well. How could we face her again afterward? But if we didn't know her, how could we be sure that she wouldn't go around telling people about it or blackmail us or something?

Then, three years ago, we took a trip to Europe. One of the cities we visited was Amsterdam. Everybody in the travel business says you haven't really seen Amsterdam unless you visit the red-light district. So we went there one evening. It wasn't hard to find. Well, I want to tell you, I've never seen anything like it.

In the United States, prostitution is something that's usually hidden behind closed doors, but not in Amsterdam. The red-light district is a part of the city specifically set aside for prostitution and erotic entertainment. The women who work there sit in their windows wearing sexy clothing and inviting the men who pass by to come in and visit. A man looking for sex can window-shop until he finds one that appeals to him. It's as simple and as straightforward as that.

For me, it was absolutely fascinating. There were all types of women there. Some tried to look like innocent young girls, wearing their hair in braids and dressing in shorts or sunsuits. Others were openly sexy, displaying themselves in brief, lacy underwear. The ones that interested me the most, though, were the classy-looking ones. They wore formal looking gowns or really fancy negligees.

The rooms were all small—just space enough for a bed and a chair. But they were all neat and clean-looking. In some, there were bright lights so that a shopper could get a good view of the merchandise. Others just had a little candle burning to present a feeling of romance. All had red bulbs outside that were turned on when the woman inside was available and turned off when she was occupied.

We walked around for about an hour, strolling up and down the narrow streets and looking into all the windows. Sometimes I felt a little awkward being there. At one point, I guess I kind of stared at one of the women. She was really cute, young and clean-looking with short blond hair and a peaches-and-cream complexion. She was wearing a long white satin nightgown that hugged her ample breasts and caressed her thighs and hips.

Suddenly, as I looked at her, she smiled and winked. Then, opening her mouth, she stuck her tongue out at me and wiggled it up and down. I thought that she was mocking me for staring at her. I got all embarrassed and hurried away, gripping Eric's arm.

But Eric laughed. "She liked you," he said. "She was inviting you inside."

At first, I thought he was nuts. It had never occurred to me that the women in the windows might be selling their services to other women. But the more I thought about it, the more I realized that he was probably right. What a deliciously exciting idea.

That night, I thought about the red-light district while I lay in bed trying to fall asleep. It was one of the most unusual places I had ever been. I decided that I wanted to go back there for another look. It would have to be the next day, because that would be our last day in Amsterdam.

When I mentioned it to Eric over breakfast, he was all for it. So, in the evening, we headed for sex town again. I wasn't actually looking for the cute blonde from the previous day, but every once in a while I thought I saw her in one of the windows. Each time it turned out I was wrong. Once, I said something to Eric. "Could that be the one that winked at me yesterday?" Something like that.

"No," he said. "She was a little farther up the block."

The streets and alleys were so winding and complicated that I really doubted Eric could remember the location. And, anyway, I wasn't particularly interested in seeing her. I wasn't even sure I would recognize her if I did. But then I looked up, and there she was smiling at me from a chair in the window. The second I saw her, I realized it was the same woman. She was even wearing the same white satin nightgown. She beckoned with her hand, looking me right in the eye and inviting me in.

Without even thinking, I turned to Eric and said, "Let's do it." All that came out was a hoarse whisper. But Eric heard it and took my hand. A moment later, we were opening the door and stepping inside a neat little room.

The woman immediately rose from her chair and closed the window shade. "I am Greta," she said. "What is your pleasure?" She spoke perfect English. She even had a British accent.

"The pleasure is for her," Eric answered, gesturing toward me.

"And you want to watch?" Greta said matter-of-factly.

"I want to help," Eric answered.

Greta looked at me and then at Eric again. "So the pleasures that I give will be just for your friend here?" she asked.

"This is my wife, Kelly," he said.

I could hear tension in Eric's voice, and I was so nervous myself that I couldn't even concentrate on what was going on.

Greta was very professional about it, though. She recognized what we wanted of her and took charge immediately. "That will be seventy-five guilders," she said, "I'll be glad to accept a traveler's check."

As soon as Greta put away the money Eric counted into her hand, she removed her nightgown. I just stood there staring at her. Her breasts were big and round. The hair on her pubic mound was much darker than the hair on her head. I didn't know what to do next.

Turning to Eric, Greta said, "Would you like to take your clothes off?"

Eric glanced at me and answered, "No. I think I'll keep them on for the time being."

As Greta walked toward me, her breasts swayed slightly from side to side. Still feeling kind of numb, I watched them, looking at her dark nipples. Without another word, she started unbuttoning my blouse and pulling it out of the waist of my pants. When it was off, she unhooked and removed my bra. I felt myself getting out of breath. I don't ever remember being so excited before.

For a moment, Greta stroked my breasts, making my nipples as hard as hers. She rolled them in her fingers until my whole body tingled with arousal. Then, taking my hands, she placed them on her breasts. It was the first time in my life that I touched another woman's naked body. I can't even begin to describe the thrill. There's no question that part of it came from having my husband right there watching me.

We stood for a while, stroking each other's breasts. Then Greta guided one of my hands to her pubic mound. At first, I just left my hand where she had placed it. But then I started to explore. I ran my fingers through the soft curls of hair. After a moment, I actually touched the moist slit of her opening. She moved her pelvis slightly, and before I knew what was happening, my fingertip was inside her.

I was in a wonderful erotic daze. It didn't feel like it was real at all. More like a dream. I honestly believed that I was going to wake up any second.

While I explored her vagina, she finished undressing me, sliding my pants and panties down over my hips and letting them fall to the floor. Then she touched my vagina the way I was touching hers. Only she did it much better. It felt like her fingers were on me and in me all at the same time, petting my clit, tantalizing my labia, stroking my mound, driving me crazy. I glanced up at Eric and saw him staring intently at the two of us. The front of his pants was like a tent over his erection.

In a husky voice, Greta said, "Kelly, why don't you lie on the bed? Your husband can stand right next to it so he'll be close by."

She led me to the bed and guided me down so that I was lying on my back. Gently, she used her hands to spread my knees and thighs. My pussy was completely open and exposed to her. She stroked it lightly with her fingers until my tissues were covered with moisture. Then she lapped softly at me with the tip of her tongue.

Eric leaned over the bed and cupped my breasts in his hands. It was better than my wildest fantasy. My husband's fingers toyed with my nipples while Greta's tongue probed my slit. I looked down to see the feminine mouth working expertly at giving pleasure to my vagina. I still couldn't believe it was happening. Reaching down, I touched Greta's hair and ears, just to confirm that she was really there.

Wanting to experience the threesome more completely, I unzipped Eric's fly and took out his cock. It was huge and harder than I ever remember it. I glanced at Greta in time to see her looking up. I was glad. I wanted her to see how big and rigid my husband's penis was. She kept licking me while she stared at it.

I started stroking Eric's cock feverishly with my hand. I think that, in part, I wanted to show it to Greta. I liked the idea of having her watch while I rubbed his penis. I jerked at it, feeling it throb in my hand while I rolled my hips to shove my pussy harder against Greta's sucking mouth.

The little room was filled with the wet sounds of her tongue plunging my depths. I knew that I was seconds away from orgasm and I wanted Eric to come with me. I started to groan to let him know how close I was. I pulled harder and more steadily on his erection. I could feel his cock getting wet as droplets of moisture oozed from its tip. We were both poised at the brink.

Then Eric shouted and his penis began to spurt. The first jet of semen struck my breast. At the same moment, Greta's tongue swabbed my clit, and my climax erupted. I kept playing with Eric's cock, spraying his come all over my body as I poured my sex juices into Greta's hungry mouth. She continued licking me until all my energy was spent and Eric's now-limp penis slipped from my grasp.

Greta kissed my pussy tenderly and said, "I enjoyed that. I hope you did too." She rose and put her nightgown back on.

I got up and started dressing. I ran a comb through my hair while Eric zipped up his fly and adjusted his clothing. As we were leaving, Greta said, "Thank you very much. Have a wonderful trip." When we were outside, she opened the shade and turned the red light back on.

It was the most erotic experience I ever had in my life. I know that Eric feels that way too. It was so comfortable for both of us. Greta never made us feel the least bit awkward. Everything seemed so perfectly natural. Maybe the fact that we were so far from home and knew that we'd never see her again was what prevented it from being threatening in any way to either of us.

Since then, our threesome fantasies have been more exciting than ever before. After all, we actually lived out the dream we had shared for so long. Now, whenever we pretend there's another woman in bed with us, it's Greta. When Eric describes the things she's doing, I can actually see and feel them. It's not just a fantasy anymore. It's a memory. We brought back a wonderful souvenir of Amsterdam—Greta!

15

Create Your Own Erotic Fantasies

The erotic fantasies described in this book are as varied as the couples who share them. Some enjoy creating imaginary situations they never really expect to experience. Others derive pleasure from whispering about events that actually have occurred or might occur in the future. Some—like the couple who pretend to be observers at the orgy room of a sex club—imagine situations they regard as kinky. Others—like the couple who dream of making love on a golf course—prefer fantasies that differ from their personal reality in detail only. One feature all their fantasies have in common is that they help to enrich the sex lives of the couples who share them.

You and your mate can also benefit from the pleasures of creating and sharing erotic fantasies. If you haven't done so already, it's high time you did. The fact that you have read this far is a sign that the idea appeals to you. If your partner has also read or is reading this book, the idea must appeal to him or her as well. Probably, you'd both like to give it a try, but neither of you knows how to begin. Once you get started, though, it's going to be a whole lot easier than you think.

The first step is to realize the role that fantasy already plays in your life. Although growing up teaches us that fantasies are kid stuff and that adults are supposed to live in a world of reality, the truth is that everybody fantasizes. A fantasy is just a picture that you see in your mind. If you can close your eyes and see the Eiffel Tower, you are fantasizing.

Most of the things you do would never get done if you didn't imagine them first, and "imagination" is simply another name for "fantasy." Every time you plan a vacation, you are imagining a week in the mountains or a month at the seashore. If you discuss these vacation plans with your spouse, you're sharing a fantasy.

Many of our fantasies are sexual. Before having sex, we imagine or fantasize about it—sometimes for hours, sometimes only for an instant. Since we all had different experiences as our sexuality was developing, we all have different fantasies.

By experimenting, you can discover what kinds of fantasy are most likely to arouse you and what kinds are most likely to arouse your spouse. Don't expect them to be identical; that's as unlikely as finding two people with the same fingerprints. With practice, though, you can combine elements to create and share mutual fantasies that will raise you both to new heights of passion and excitement.

Some of the common elements of sexual fantasy described in the chapters of this book may furnish your material. You and your spouse may build erotic fantasies around memories of a particular sex experience you had together, or even of an experience one of you had without the other. If you like sexy books or movies, you might improvise on scenes you both find especially arousing. You may learn that both of you have sexual thoughts when engaging in certain nonsexual activities—like playing golf or checking into a motel. If so, you can use those thoughts as the foundation for erotic fantasies you share.

Obviously, there are some activities that are better in fantasy than they would be in reality. It might be great fun to imagine vacationing in the Amazon jungle, for example, even though the reality of such a trip is likely to include insect bites and malaria. Similarly, there are probably some sexual activities that you and your spouse would not really enjoy doing, but that you might both love fantasizing about.

This means that in selecting a fantasy to share, you don't have to rule anything out. It might be that if you and your spouse really tried to make love in a public place you'd both be so embarrassed you would lose your desire. In spite of this, however, you might find that imagining sex before an audience of thousands in Yankee Stadium turns you both on. If it does, you can experience it in a shared fantasy that includes all the excitement and pleasure while eliminating the shame. Many of the couples who contributed to this book said that they would never consider doing the things they fantasized about. That didn't stop them, though, from enjoying the fantasy.

Fantasy-sharing is a joint venture, and success in any joint venture requires cooperation. It may take a bit of daring to get this kind of venture started, but you'll probably decide that it's worth the effort. Many of the people to whom we spoke said that at first they feared that their spouses would refuse to join in their flights of erotic imagination. In the long run, however, all found their mates to be willing participants.

You may already be sharing fantasies. Or you may both look up from this book at precisely the same instant and simultaneously say, "Let's try it." If so, the rest is easy. If not, you can take active steps to get started. Once you do, you will probably discover that your partner has a more elaborate and more flexible imagination than you realized.

If fantasy-sharing is a new experience for you, it might be best to start with something simple and safe. After you have explored your partner's secret thoughts, the two of you may end up creating fantasies so wild and kinky that you'd never think of telling us about them. In the beginning, however, concentrate on what you already know about your mate.

Think of a sexual experience which you had together and about which the two of you enjoy reminiscing. Mention it when you and your partner are feeling sexy. If the memory makes you both feel sexier, talk about it for a while. As the pleasant feelings continue, embellish the memory a little by imagining something that could have made the experience even more exciting. At this point, it doesn't matter whether you do all the talking or whether you and your mate are taking turns; the fantasy-sharing has begun.

There is no need to say or do anything that makes either of you feel awkward. Some of the couples in this book whisper words to each other that they would never use outside their bedrooms. Others are more conservative, even in their secret whispers. When sharing erotic descriptions, be as clinically explicit or as romantically poetic as you like. Nobody is there but the two of you.

In time, you may find that even the most casual conversation can lead to fantasy-sharing. A husband who tells his wife that the dress she's wearing looks terrific might go on to say something about crawling under it to do sexy things. A wife who compliments her husband's golf swing might end up talking about games the two of them could play if they had the clubhouse shower room all to themselves.

Remember that the fantasies you share are not necessarily descriptions of things that either of you would actually like to do. They are daydreams, nothing more. You've both been having them anyway, and they haven't damaged your relationship. Sharing them won't cause harm as long as you accept your partner's fantasies without resentment and share your own without guilt or embarrassment. As you both become more comfortable whispering your secret thoughts, inhibitions that once blocked total communication will be relaxed. As a result, you and your spouse will learn things about yourselves and each other that you never knew.

Before long, you will accumulate a repertoire of fantasies for sharing. Probably, each of you will experiment with erotic images to add to existing fantasies or to use as the basis for new ones. When this happens, it is important for you to let each other know how you feel about the new ideas. Watch each other to see whether the element most recently introduced has an arousing effect. Be sensitive to turn-offs as well as turn-ons.

It isn't necessary for you to participate equally in the telling and listening. In some couples, one partner always does the talking, while in others the partners change roles. Whether you are giving or receiving, the most important thing is communication. When your spouse is describing a fantasy, let him or her know which parts of the description you like and which parts you don't. When you do the whispering, be ready to change direction at the first sign of discomfort in your mate.

Fantasies are pictures that exist in the mind. Your fantasy is your picture. Try to choose words that will give your partner an image as vivid as your own. It isn't necessary for him or her to see exactly what you see as long as you both feel the same kind of excitement.

Let fantasy-sharing become a form of sexual foreplay that you can enjoy in or out of the bedroom. When you are describing erotic images to each other in the car on the way to dinner, none of the people in the vehicles around you will have any idea what you're up to. You can continue the conversation over a table in a restaurant and return to it on the way back home. You can keep it up while you're undressing and slipping under the covers. You don't really have to stop until you want to.

Sooner or later, it will occur to one or both of you that it might be fun to act out one of your favorite fantasies. As couples in the previous chapter have discovered, that kind of experiment can be blissful or disastrous. Think carefully and talk candidly before attempting to live out a fantasy.

There are some things that you would both like to do but can't because of circumstances beyond your control. Then fantasy-sharing becomes a substitute for the unattainable reality. You might love the idea of sex in your backyard swimming pool, for example, but never do it because of your nosy neighbors. If your neighbors suddenly leave town or some other change in circumstances permits you to act out your imaginary experience, the reality may be even more exciting than the fantasy.

Remember, though, it isn't always easy to predict how you or your spouse will react to a particular experience. Some fantasies are based on things that neither of you would really enjoy doing at all. Sharing these fantasies allows you to experience the pleasures of such activities without being damaged by their negative aspects. The thought of participating in an orgy with dozens of strangers might be quite exciting, for example, even though you would be horrified to actually see your spouse having sex with another person. Acting out this kind of fantasy can devastate your relationship.

In fantasy, everything always turns out the way we want it to. We are in control. If our imagination takes an unwanted turn, we can blink away a detail and replace it with another. Reality, however, is not so easily manipulated. Once a boulder begins to roll, it may be difficult to make it stop. Before attempting to actualize a fantasy experience, partners should thoroughly explore each other's attitudes. If there is any possibility that living out a sexual fantasy will cause discomfort for either partner, the idea should be postponed or abandoned.

Acting it out can be even better than fantasizing about it, but only if both partners feel that way. To be sure that they will, partners should thoroughly discuss in advance all aspects of the reality and their feelings about it. This discussion should not take place while fantasizing or having sex, but in the cold light of day, when passion is less likely to overcome reason. Even then, it should be understood that either partner can have a change of heart and call it off at any time—even after the real-life action has begun.

In addition, some thought should be given to details of reality that cannot be blinked away. A dream of making love in a grassy meadow can be beautiful as long as there are no ants in the dream. There are sure to be some in the grass, though.

Be careful. Acting out your fantasies can be risky. Before taking that kind of risk, talk about it. Be sure it's something you both really want to do. Be sure, also, that you understand the difference between reality and imagination.

There's no risk in having fantasies, though, or in sharing them with someone you love. The collection in this book can get you started. Try selecting one that you especially like, and asking your mate whether it also appeals to him or her. Talk about it while reading it together. Don't just summarize or paraphrase it, but say why it turns you on and encourage your partner to do so too. If you trust each other enough, you will both begin improvising on it, tailoring it to your mutual tastes. Eventually, it may become one of your own whispered secrets.

Here is one of ours.

* * *

Our erotic fiction has attracted the attention of a militant group of terrorists who have kidnapped us and brought us to their stronghold in the forest. They are advocates of free love and are planning to overthrow our present form of government and replace it with a sexocracy. Their camp in the woods is like something out of Robin Hood, with tables at which dozens of naked people are seated, feasting. Wine flows freely from oak barrels.

We have been placed in a large cage in the middle of the clearing and our clothes have been taken from us. We lie helpless on the floor of our cage, on naked display for the enjoyment of our captors. Several nude men and women approach the cage laughing lustfully. One of the women presses her face against the bars and stares at us, licking her lips. Her breasts are huge, with brown nipples that immediately swell to erection.

One of the men steps up behind her, pressing his penis between her buttocks as his arms encircle her. He takes her breasts in his hands and begins manipulating them, rolling the dark rubbery tips in his fingers. She sighs, shoving her ass against him and reaching between her thighs to fondle his scrotum.

Another man peers into the cage and rubs his own manhood as he walks toward the writhing couple. He continues stroking himself with one hand while his other begins petting the woman's hairy pubic mound. Slowly, she sinks to the ground, pulling the second man on top of her. We watch as she takes his penis in her hand and guides it into her waiting vulva.

As soon as he is inside her, he begins pumping his hips back and forth, driving his erection deeper and deeper into her. A moment later, they roll over so that she is on top, her round white ass waving erotically in the air. The other man drops to his knees behind her and spreads her buttocks wide, exposing the moist dark crack of her anus.

He inches forward, placing the tip of his swollen organ against the tight orifice and grinding his hips in tight circles. We see him sliding it into her anal opening a millimeter at a time. When the head is completely inside her, he hunches forward, embedding his entire length in her bowel with one quick thrust. She gasps in ecstasy as all three of them rock to the rhythm of panting desire.

As their bodies fuse, other groups of terrorists begin drifting toward the cage. Looking from us to the gyrating threesome, they come together sexually in groups of two, three, four, and even five. Mouths and genitals meet in every imaginable combination. The air is filled with their cries and the fragrances of their passion. Even though we are caged captives, we cannot help but share in their contagious excitement.

The revelers watch one another as they indulge their wildest desires. Every group becomes infected with the arousal of every other group. They seem to be performing for one another as much as for themselves. They are masters of the art of sexual pleasure and erotic exhibition.

While the others roll about the ground in passionate embrace, their leader steps up to the cage. He is tall and powerful, with a massive throbbing erection. "Your only hope of leaving here," he says, "is to entertain us. You've got to give us a show even better than the one we're giving you. If you don't, you'll be our slaves forever. If you do, we'll set you free."